Unlock the Blocks

Unlock the Blocks

25 KEYS TO INCREASE YOUR CREATIVITY, PRODUCTIVITY AND SELF-ESTEEM

Rachel *"Doc Hollywood"* Ballon, Ph.D.

WRITE WORD PRESS
Los Angeles, California

Published by Write Word Press
Los Angeles, California
ISBN: 0983845115
ISBN: 9780983845119

J I H G F E D C B A
Library of Congress Cataloging-in-Publication Data
Ballon, Rachel
Unlock the Blocks / Rachel Ballon.

1. Writer's block—Handbooks, manuals, etc.
2. Authors—Mental health—Handbooks, manuals, etc

Library of Congress Control Number: 2015950247
Write Word Press, Los Angeles, CA

Acknowledgements

To the many clients, and students who encouraged me to republish my original book. Thank you to those artists, musicians, dancers, executives, and all creative individuals, who saw the value in Ballon Method Writing™ and suggested not to limit it only to writers, but to realize that all creative professional would benefit from the information and the exercises. I especially want to thank Lisa Lieberman Doctor whose own creativity inspired me to update and re-release this book. It is now opened to all who are blocked in their lives, careers, or relationships.

Dediction

To my five grandchildren—Bradley, Brittany, Jacob, Brandon and Julien—your free spirit, creativity and imagination are awe-inspiring.

Table of Contents

Introduction

"Planning to write is not writing. Outlining... researching... talking to people about what you're doing, none of that is writing. Writing is writing."
—E. L. DOCTOROW

*U*nlock The Blocks offers you the opportunity to carry your own personal therapist in your hip pocket, handbag, or backpack, the goal of encouraging and supporting you throughout your writing challenges and of releasing your creativity. As a California licensed psychotherapist—in private practice for over thirty years—who is also a writing teacher, a creativity coach, and international writing consultant, I specialize in working with writers and creative professionals on personal and professional issues such as overcoming blocks, fear of rejection, self-doubt, and procrastination, as well as increasing productivity and creativity.

I know first-hand that as an artist, you need all the support you can get. I've counseled thousands of writers, from experienced professionals to rank beginners, and am familiar with their pain as well as their joy; their self-doubt as well as their self-expression; and their critical as well as their creative selves.

As a writer, you often work in a vacuum, alone and isolated, without any guarantee your writing will be published, produced, or sold. I've treated writers who have become discouraged and felt like giving up, but who kept going and worked through their negativity. Others did give up their dreams. How sad!!!

It takes courage and commitment to continue writing despite feelings of failure, self-criticism and repeated rejection. At writers' conferences throughout the United States and Europe, where I've spoken as both a writers' psychotherapist and a coach, I've heard the stories about the pain of the creative life. Many writers have asked me to help them with not being able to write and feelings of paralysis. Others wanted advice on personal issues. Still others suffered from feelings of self-doubt and low self-esteem.

Unfortunately, time was limited at these conferences, and it was impossible to give more than a little encouragement in the space of a five-minute conversation. I've always wished I could give other writers the tools and techniques I have given my clients in my private practice, tools that have proved to be successful as well as easy to implement. I wanted to offer the same successful work I've done with my clients to all of you who have artistic blocks and are looking for solutions. I'm excited about finally making this material available to you so that you, too, can experience positive remedies to pervasive problems that deplete your creative energy and your creative spirit, whether you're a writer or not.

Unlock the Blocks is your own personal therapist and coach in a book. Now you won't have to worry; you have all the support and help you could possibly need right at your fingertips. This book not only provides you with encouragement, comfort, and nurturing, it also allows you to discover the secrets of creativity-- getting started, overcoming procrastination, fear of rejection and perfectionism. It will help you explore the core problems beneath your symptoms, as you get to the root of your obstacles and become reconnected to your Creative Source.

In the process of reading this book and doing the writing exercises, you will have the opportunity to clearly identify what's stopping you and your own creativity. You will most definitely discover a satisfying solution for overcoming your personal obstacles and be well on your way to working again.

There are as many different causes of blocks as there are writers. Writing is hard work. As a licensed psychotherapist, I work with all types of writers and creative professionals on every level. In my private practice, I have dealt with every kind of personal, professional, and psychological problem that they experience.

When creatives feel discouraged, depressed, or demoralized, it's often the result of outside circumstances such as not being able to get work, not being able to sell the work, not being able to make a living through their art, or not being able to get an agent. Rather than focus on these problems, my clients and I work on solutions. Together, we develop personal action plans and set creative goals. We search for successful strategies to be proactive rather than inactive. We also work together to raise self-esteem and to transform negative, self-defeating beliefs into positive ones

Do You Believe in Your Writing and in Yourself?

In many instances, I've motivated, encouraged, and inspired writers who didn't believe in themselves or in their talent to honor their creative abilities. When clients come to see me with these particular issues, I don't spend too much time looking at their blocks; instead, I spend our time together coaching them to develop specific strategies to get back on the right track again.

I know that helping you change your negative beliefs into positive ones and giving you solutions to attain the right frame of mind are the most important ways I can help you stop staring at the same blank page every day and start writing.

I've encountered all the negative attitudes, from "I'm not good enough" to "I should get a real job" to "I really have nothing new to say." These self-defeating thoughts can immobilize you and gnaw at your spirit until you give up.

What about you? Do you tend to think this way about yourself and your work? Are you able to keep on going, even after you've been rejected? Or are you like the many creative individuals, who have little faith in their artistic abilities and sometimes even less faith in themselves?

That is the main reason I wrote this book. My goal is to help you, no matter what kind of blocks you suffer—whether it's negative thinking or insecurity, creativity crisis or psychological barriers or personal fears—and give you solutions to your problems. My purpose is to share the methods that are proven to overcome these obstacles and help you become a self-motivated and productive person.

Your Own Portable Therapist, for Support Wherever You Go

Unlock the Blocks is unique in its focus and intent, which is to provide encouragement to anyone who wants or needs support during the course of the creative journey. You can easily take this book with you wherever you go to help you make detours around creative roadblocks and show you how to jump over creative hurdles. This book offers you the means of achieving the same positive results in your writing that clients have experienced in my private practice; you, too, can experience the beautiful works you were born to create. Throughout reading this book, you'll overcome your blocks and learn how to develop the enthusiasm and energy to defeat personal frustrations and fears. Take *Unlock the Blocks* along with you and always keep it within reach. Its only as far away as your fingertips, your own personal psychotherapist and coach, ready to cheer you on, cheer you up, encourage you, inspire you, and motivate you when you feel you can't write another word or aren't a good enough talent in the first place.

Sometimes you might feel you have neither the inner resources nor the confidence to stay motivated. Just as professional athletes need a coach to give them strategies for winning, creative people also need a coach to give them strategies to win the creativity game. And just as athletes have a sports psychologist to talk to when the coach isn't able to help them overcome their lack of confidence or bad case of nerves, you also need to discover what's preventing you from creating your best or even creating at all.

Is It the Writer or the Writing?

The creative problems discussed in this book are the roadblocks that most commonly stop artists. If you've ever encountered one of these obstacles, you know that they can prevent you from being all you can be in your career.

Through *Unlock the Blocks*, I will help you break free of the obstacles and problems that keep you from writing, so that you realize your full creative potential as a talented, productive, and successful person.

You must go within to understand your symptoms of procrastination as well as your fears. This is especially true in cases where these creative problems aren't obvious. At these times you need the assistance of a psychotherapist to help you discover the real hidden causes that are keeping you blocked. More often than not these blocks aren't about the writing at all; rather, it's the person him- or herself who might be psychologically blocked. Through the pages of this book, I act as just that: the therapist and creativity coach you need, ready and able to provide answers and remedies for your various creative difficulties, whether they're internal or external. Just as importantly, I can provide you with the motivation and inspiration that will help you to Unlock the Blocks.

Because I wear two professional hats—that of a psychotherapist and of a writing coach—I have the ability to discern whether the problem you are experiencing is with you or with your writing. Let me explain what I mean. Let's say you were one of my clients in my private practice. You had come to me in need of help with your script. You tell me you're blocked. Now, after speaking with you, I am in the unique position of being able to make a proper diagnosis. I can determine whether it's you, who is blocked, or does your problem lie within your craft. If I were just a writing coach, I'd read your script, figure out what was wrong with it, and tell you how you could fix it. We'd discuss your writing and hopefully solve your problem. However, chances are you'd still be unable to complete your script. Why? Because the block does not have anything to do with your script, but everything to do with you!

As you can see, if I weren't a psychotherapist, I wouldn't have the tools or the training to arrive at the conclusion that the problem was something internal, having to do with you as an individual more than with your work. Without this kind of specialized assistance, you would still be stuck in your block. You could continue to go from consultant to consultant and never resolve your real block. As an artist, I'm sure you can understand how important it is for the person you go to for help is capable of correctly diagnosing the root cause that is stopping you from working. The reasons could stem from a variety of sources: emotional or structural, psychological or personal, creative or craft.

Making the Proper Diagnosis Is the Key to Creativity

So when a client comes to me complaining of being blocked, the first thing I always do is ask that one question: Is it your work or is it you? The answer to that question helps me make a proper diagnosis, and then I am able to help the person overcome the creative obstacle. These obstacles can have a myriad of causes, whether it is fear of rejection or lack of skills; fear of failure or no knowledge of structure; fear of success or not knowing how to write a story. I can only help you find the right solution after the problem is correctly diagnosed. Rather than just dealing with the presenting symptoms, such as procrastination, or perfectionism, it is necessary to dig out the real problem and its root cause. As we work together throughout this book, I will help you discover what's stopping you so that you can then proceed with your work and your creative journey.

From Individual Sessions to Creative Solutions

Unlock the Blocks is based on actual sessions I've had with clients over the past thirty years. These sessions share a common focus, not only in terms of the problem presented by individuals, but in terms of the solutions clients found to overcome these problems. The focus, therefore, is on finding working solutions to various creative and artistic problems—issues that you could encounter in your own creative life.

I've condensed thousands of sessions, down to the 25 that represent the most common and prevalent reasons why creative artists don't create. Instead of chapters, therefore, this book is composed of "sessions." These sessions are intended to feature the major aspects and areas of a typical creative problem. Some of the sessions are based on the writers' support groups that I conduct. As with any support group, individuals in these groups discuss issues, problems, and conflicts that relate to everyone in the group. In reading each session, you'll discover solutions to your own personal obstacles and blocks.

In the process of condensing these individual sessions, I've also encapsulated the long periods of time clients had to work on their specific blocks. As a result, the problems presented in these sessions take much less time to resolve than it often took clients to resolve in real time. Moreover, they give you the benefit of learning from all the other artists who experienced long-term work and self-exploration. Because many of these issues are so closely related, some sessions in the book may seem to overlap. For example, low self-esteem and fear of rejection are similar and yet very different. You might wonder if they could be combined, but the origins of these problems are as varied as the individuals who experienced them. The root causes are different. The individuals featured in each session are as different as each of you is different. No matter how similar these problems may seem, it really is necessary to deal with each one individually.

These sessions depict writers from the most professional to the most inexperienced beginner, all of whom have suffered from and overcame the blocks to creativity that are dealt with in this book. The "clients" used as examples throughout the book are really composites of clients I've treated throughout the years. They are representative of the most difficult problems and common challenges besetting writers of all genres. The names of clients in the sessions are fictitious, and any resemblance to a real person is purely coincidental.

As you read this book, imagine you're a client in my private practice coming to talk about your problem. Pretend that you're having a session with me and we're exploring what's stopping you. Imagine yourself sitting in my office as we work together until we find a solution to your creative problem. Through reading this book and doing the writing exercises, you'll discover how to identify your personal obstacles and professional creative problems. More importantly, with my guidance every step of the way, you'll learn how to enhance your creativity and experience success. I'll show you how to set personal goals and successfully reach them; conquer your insecurity about creating; and overcome hurdles by giving up your self-defeating thoughts and behaviors.

Unlock the Blocks offers you strategies for getting inspiration when you're feeling uninspired; hope when you're feeling hopeless, and motivation when you're feeling unmotivated. This book offers more than words of encouragement. It offers you solutions to demoralizing self-doubt, along with specific techniques that will keep you on track and focused on your goals and artistic gifts. Happy journey!

SESSION 1

Getting It Started: Let It Flow, Let it Flow, Let it Flow

"Stretch your mind and fly."
—AFRICAN PROVERB

Flow. It's the state to which every writer aspires, the state immortalized in film, after film, the state in which the writer writes passionately, brilliantly, and unhesitatingly, as if the words were channeled straight from heaven itself.

You can write this way. You can write this way now. I'm going to show you how, in this, our first session together.

I had an epiphany during the writing of this book. On the surface, it has always seemed that the essence of my work with writers and creative professionals is to help them increase their creativity while decreasing their creative and psychological blocks. However, I realized, my work has another, deeper benefit. Although, it is true that I give clients the tools to increase their productivity, the real value of these tools is the ability they give my clients to actually heal themselves through their writing.

If it sounds strange to you that writing should be a means of healing, remember that I am a licensed psychotherapist—and clients who I work with, whether in person by phone or via the internet, could be said to be looking for a way to heal their wounded creative psyches. Take that idea one step further, and you'll see that writing itself is a means of healing. Writing allows you to access blocked emotions, pent-up pain, and buried anger and then release those feelings onto the page. The pen is a powerful tool for liberating you and your creative potential from the tyranny of dormant negative emotions, which are the real barriers to your talent and creativity.

By releasing old, negative, blocked emotions, you almost literally open up to make room inside of yourself for new feelings and capabilities. The benefits of cleaning your emotional slate and opening yourself to your inner creative resources are many: You'll feel more hopeful than fearful, more helpful than helpless, and more productive than paralyzed. You will also become a more passionate and powerful writer. Through the process of this book and completing the exercises, which are proven methods, you will gain the ability to clearly identify what's stopping you and your creativity. And you will most definitely discover a satisfying solution for overcoming your blocks and be well on your way to being productive again.

The following sections describe the means by which this book helps you overcome those obstacles. You'll read about the Ballon Method Writing,™ and learn about the Creativity Chronicles. Together these methods, techniques, and exercises will enable you to experience the same benefit as clients in my private practice—it will be as though you're in a session with me, "on the couch."

Ballon Method Writing™

"Write freely and as rapidly as possible and throw the whole thing on paper. Never correct or rewrite until the whole thing is down."
—*JOHN STEINBECK*

For many years I have been conducting creativity workshops for writers, producers, directors, actors, and other creative professionals throughout the world. It was during the course of these many workshops that I developed the techniques for a powerful way of writing called Ballon Method Writing.™ This Method creates fast flow writing:

Free	Feeling
Authentic	Liberate
Spontaneous	Open
Transformative	Wonder

Ballon Method Writing™ is easy to learn because it comes straight from the heart. It's simple, but not simplistic, and the results are all-powerful and emotional. When you use it you'll produce the best writing ever in the space of only twenty minutes. In my personal experience with thousands of writers to whom I've taught this Method, it enables you to unlock the blocks, overcome writing fears, be in the flow, bypass the inner critics, and open the door to unlimited creativity. You'll realize your creative potential by using this method as you work the Creativity Chronicle exercises throughout this book.

Ballon Method Writing™ allows you to be present in your writing process without judgment. It enables you to be the creative person you were always meant to be by letting your writing flow from your heart to the page without analysis. The way to achieve all the benefits of this method is through learning the elements that are the basis of it. By following them your writing will be heartfelt and honest; passionate and powerful; sensual and strong; emotional and energized.

Start with the Magic Numbers 5....3.....7

Ballon Method Writing™ is based on the concept that in order to write well and freely, you must first take the time to prepare yourself ready to write. Pick out a favorite place where you can make yourself comfortable and where you can count on some uninterrupted private time. This might be your creative space in your own home or another place where you feel relaxed and serene. Once you are comfortable, close your eyes and concentrate on your breathing. If you like, you can play some of your favorite music, as long as it is conducive to achieving a state of relaxation— something quiet, like New Age music or Classical music will work best.

The magic numbers are 5...3....7. As you breathe in, slowly count to five. Hold that breath to the count of three (the second magic number). Breathe out more slowly, to the count of seven. Continue breathing in this rhythm for at least five minutes. Focus your awareness on your body; you should feel more relaxed as you continue deep breathing. Just remember to follow your breath to the count of five–three–seven, throughout the process.

Visualize and Imagine

After a short while, your breathing will follow the 5–3–7 pattern naturally. Now it's time to add a visual element to the relaxation process. Visualize a favorite place. This can be anything, real or imagined that makes you feel positive and peaceful. Fill this picture in your mind's eye with colorful details. This technique, known as visualization, is a powerful technique for enhancing your creativity—literally! By focusing on strong mental images, you slowly filter out input from the left side of your brain (the logical, practical side). This leaves you free to pay better attention to images from the right side of your brain, the site associated with artistic creativity. Visualize the scene with your five senses of touch, tastes, sound, sight and smell.

Before sitting down to begin any of these exercises, be sure to implement this process of relaxation, deep breathing, and visualization, first.

Using Ballon Method Writing™

Once you relax and awaken the creative side of your brain with your visualization exercise, you're ready to begin writing using Ballon Method Writing.™ Your goal here is to write as fast as you can without stopping for a full twenty minutes. This is a must. Don't take the pen from the page, and keep it moving until the allotted twenty minutes are up.

At some point, especially when you're new to this Method, you may feel as though you have run out of things to write long before twenty minutes. Keep writing anyway! What you write doesn't matter as much as that you write as rapidly as you can. If you can't think of anything more to write then continue by writing down your thoughts and feelings in the moment. For example you might write, "I wish I could stop writing. My hand is tired and I have nothing more to write." Just keep writing as fast as you can, and no matter what don't stop writing until the allotted time is up.

All of the writing should be in the first person and in present tense. Instead of writing about the past—"I wanted my red balloon back"— puts you back in that time you're recalling your past. So write in the present: "I want my red balloon." You need to be present in your scene; in this way, you will be better able to re-experience your past emotions in your present writing. Capture every sensory detail of your memory. What do you see? Feel? Taste? Hear? Smell? Touch? By re-creating a past experience as completely as you can through your five senses, you're able to release any negative emotions associated with it. This allows you to break free from the blocks that resulted from those painful feelings and open yourself to new, positive, powerful feelings of creativity.

There's no such thing as wrong writing during this process. Don't concern yourself with grammar, spelling, vocabulary, punctuation or sentence structure. All of those are left–brain tasks, and the more you worry about them, the more your right–brain creative impulses will be stifled. All you have to do is write as fast as you're physically able. Just write. Don't think. Don't analyze. Don't worry. Don't fret. Just write until you've written for twenty minutes and not one minute less. If you feel like it, you can keep writing as long as you want.

When you write using the Ballon Method Writing™ you will access a part of yourself that experiences the world of wonder and delight rather than with preset expectations and criticism. This is your "free child," to which you can feel the wonderment of your child's mind. You'll be open and spontaneous, and your writing will be liberating and authentic. The honesty of writing without following rules will enable you to lift the shackles of your own critical self and write with freedom. You'll experience a positive transformation in yourself and your writing.

Creativity Chronicle

"Creativity is a type of learning process where the teacher and the pupil are located in the same individual."
—ARTHUR KOESTLER

Each session in this book ends with a section called a Creativity Chronicle. These are exercises I created specifically for this book, with the purpose of giving you a way of reconnecting with your free child and increasing your creativity. The exercises, suggestions, and actions that comprise each Creativity Chronicle are provided to enable you to access your own creativity by going deeper within your creative self. Each is designed to be completed using Ballon Method Writing. All you need is your favorite pen and paper (computers are discouraged) and at least twenty minutes of uninterrupted private time.

In over thirty years of private practice I've discovered a set of problems and issues that tend to accompany most obstacles and blocks. After an individual session with clients, I give them writing exercises that relate to the present problems they've just discussed. Similarly, each of the Creativity Chronicles presented here relate back to the issue of the proceeding "session," whether it's self-defeating beliefs or fear of rejection. In this way it is possible for you to have the same type of experience in this book that my clients experience "on the couch."

By completing these Creativity Chronicles you make your reading experience an interactive one. You'll not only read the information, you'll also have the opportunity after every session to writing your personal Creativity Chronicle. This allows you to be proactive and experience firsthand the healing effects of Ballon Method Writing™ and the specific benefits these writing exercises have on increasing your creativity.

Wherever you take *Unlock the Blocks,* you should also have your Creativity Chronicle at your fingertips. You'll be able to use either or both whenever you wish. Sometimes, you may not feel like reading and instead just want to write. At other times you may only want to read. It's your choice. You can do these exercises anywhere you like, whenever you feel like being creative—in the park, at the beach, or in a coffeehouse.

By making a habit of writing in your Creativity Chronicle you'll begin to experience increased creativity and productivity. This will allow you to transform your blocks into promises, your obstacles into creative opportunities.

Remember, you need to use Ballon Method Writing™ as you perform the exercises given in the Creativity Chronicle. By following this method of writing you'll release your truths, write from your inner self, and let the words flow from your unconscious. There're some writers who've even had their writing exercise published just as written in class in twenty minutes, without changing a word. Isn't that amazing? No agonizing or analyzing, no rewriting or rehashing—just writing the perfect piece.

Creativity Chronicle

"The world of imagination is boundless."
—JEAN JACQUES ROUSSEAU

Recall a time in your childhood when you were in a favorite outdoor place. Maybe you were at the beach or on a lake. Perhaps you were camping in the woods or hiking in the mountains. Whatever setting you recall, be there with your five senses: touch, taste, sight, sound, and smell.

Before you write, visualize the scene. Picture what your favorite place looks like, down to the smallest detail. Imagine being completely in the scene and touching the texture of the tree bark or a grain of sand. Smell the sea air or the flowers and see the colors of the ocean or the green of the trees. Taste the salt water or the sap from a tree. Listen to the crashing of the waves or the rustling of the wind through the trees.

After you've visualized the scene and recalled the experience, pick up your pen and write about the scene. Describe what you felt with all of your senses of touch, taste, sound, sight, and smell. Use the first person (I) and present tense (am). Remember not to stop writing and write as fast as you can without lifting your pen from the page.

SHRINK WRAP-UP: UNTIL NEXT TIME

- Let the writing flow as fast as you can go.
- Write in your Creativity Chronicle every day.
- Keep the pen on the page, and don't edit and don't rewrite.

SESSION 2

Celebrating Creativity—
The Creativity Cure

"Creativity requires the courage to let go of certainties."
—ERICH FROMM

D o you wonder where your ideas come from? Have you written from your creativity? If the answer is no, it's important for you to understand the nature of creativity and its uses. Only then can you discover how to access it in order to write sizzling stories and create colorful characters; paint with passion; sing with soul.

What Is Creativity?

Do you know what creativity is? Creativity is the source of all art--including poetry, art, drama, music, and thinking out of the box. It touches people on a deep emotional level. Creativity is also free-flowing energy. When you are connected to your own inner resources, where your creativity resides, you will discover a myriad of ideas for your craft.

It's necessary for you to learn how to make your creativity available at the beginning of your project. Without creative ideas, concepts, or thoughts, you have nothing to write about and are unable to start. When you tap into your creativity, your writing is deeper and has greater dimension than when you don't connect to it.

I'll give you an example of how writing from your creativity can be a wonderful experience. It happened to me years ago, when I decided I wanted to write a screenplay. I signed up for the only daytime screenwriting class offered at UCLA extension and missed the first class. At the second class I was nervous because I knew nothing about screenwriting. We were given an assignment to write a scene for the following week.

With no book to refer to, and not knowing what I had missed, I waited until the night before the class to write my scene. I finally mustered up all my courage and started writing my scene, even though I didn't know anything about screenwriting. But what I did know was an incident concerning my dearest friend who had cancer. Digging deep inside, I plunged in and wrote a hospital scene in which a husband doesn't want to tell his wife that her tests have come back and the prognosis isn't good, even while she insists on knowing.

With much trepidation I turned in my scene the following week. I wasn't sure if I was even going to return. But the next week I did come back. In front of the entire class, the teacher asked, "Who is Rachel Ballon?"

I slowly raised my hand expecting to be ordered to leave the class because of my poor writing performance. Instead, much to my dismay, the teacher, Alfred Brenner, read my scene to the entire class, and when he was finished the class burst into applause. I was in shock. They loved it! He then proceeded to tell the class why this was such a good piece of writing. It had emotion, conflict, great dialogue, and most of all it was filled with subtext, tension, and heart.

I couldn't believe it as I left the class walking on words. I thought, "Screenwriting is a cinch. It's so easy!" Well, my early success turned out to be a fluke. Years later, after writing many screenplays, several of which were optioned by major studios, having television produced credits on ABC and becoming a member of the Writers Guild of America, I never duplicated that experience again. Never!

I'm sure it sounds surprising that instead of writing scenes better than my very first one, when I didn't know what I was doing, I haven't. Well, do you know why? It's because unconsciously, when I wrote that first scene, I wasn't attached to rules, and I allowed my creativity to flow. The scene was written from my heart, and I was in the process of being one with my writing. I had let my imagination flow down my fingertips through the pen onto the page, because I'd tapped into my creativity. It was a magical, beautiful and peak experience. That's what celebrating your creativity is. It is a fantastic, exhilarating experience and one that produces powerful, emotional, and energized writing, filled with color, movement, and humanity. Hopefully, you'll be able to write from this place after you learn how to unlock your creativity and release its power.

Creativity

"Happiness lies in the joy of achievement and the thrill of creative effort."
—*FRANKLIN D. ROOSEVELT*

As Thomas Edison once famously remarked, creativity is made up of two parts: inspiration and perspiration. As a writer, you need to discover how to combine your inspiration, or primary creativity, with your perspiration, or secondary creativity. Both aspects are necessary for you to truly be creative.

The Balance Between Primary and Secondary Creativity

Primary creativity comes from your unconscious and the right hemisphere of your brain. It is a resource for all new ideas and insights. It's where your art, inspiration, and imagination live. Without creative ideas, there are no books, art, or music. Nevertheless, as powerful as primary creativity is, it only makes up 10 percent of your creativity.

Secondary creativity emerges from the left hemisphere, and—surprisingly—it accounts for 10 percent of your creativity. It involves editing, discipline, logic, structure, analysis, rewriting, and order. This doesn't sound like the way we like to think of creativity, but it's true. To become a complete creative writer, you need both aspects of the creative process.

You want to maintain a balance between these two aspects of your creativity to access it readily. When you were a child, you easily allowed the fusion of primary and secondary creativity inside you. Unfortunately, you lost this capacity for an easy balance when, as an adult, you had already learned to hide your true self.

Combining Creativity with Craft

The same is true for your writing, art or career. Maybe you have easy access to your primary creativity and can come up with more ideas than you know what to do with, but you don't know how to put those ideas together into a solid story. When this happens, your work will fall apart. On the other hand, if you are only in touch with your secondary creativity, you may understand structure, but you won't be able to think of anything new ideas. You must have equal respect for craft, which is necessary to transform your ephemeral ideas into a strong story, painting, or strategy.

Unfortunately, I've worked with many clients who aren't able to think of any ideas and become very frustrated. Does this happen to you? Do you tell yourself that you just don't have anything exciting to write about and try to find a story that interests you outside of yourself? Well, the problem isn't that you have nothing to write; instead, it's most likely that you've closed off your own creativity.

This happens frequently when you can't channel your creativity. It's because you're not allowing your creative juices to flow. Many times you're just too analytical, too rigid, and too removed from your inner creative source.

Reconnecting to Your Free Child

To become more creative you need to have the courage to reconnect to your childhood memories and to return to those times when you were freer and less self-conscious than you are now. As you first begin to write, allow your spontaneous creative side to emerge through your words, using Ballon Method Writing.™

In the following Creativity Chronicle exercise, allow yourself the opportunity to become a playful, joyous child, to be courageous and not afraid, to let go and have fun with your writing. By permitting your child to come out and play, you'll be less judgmental, constricted, and rigid about your writing, and the words will flow onto the page in torrents.

Moving On

From this point on, you will learn about a different case study that relates to the issue at hand. Each session will help you focus on your particular area of concern regarding your own creativity. Through reading, writing, and contemplating, you'll learn the process that will lead to progress in your work and in your creative life

Creativity Chronicle

"Visualize this thing you want. See it, feel it, believe in it.
Make your mental blueprint and begin."
—ROBERT COLLIER

Visualize a wonderful place from your childhood where you felt free and spontaneous. Remember a time when, as a little child, you felt playful and alive in the world. As you visualize your scene, become part of it with all of your senses. Smell the air, look at the blue sky, and hear the music or the sound of water. Notice the myriad colors and see the different shapes and objects, whether you are indoors or outdoors. Just be one with your free child and recall the feelings you have had of being free and courageous, spontaneous and playful, fearless and joyful.

What are you wearing? How does your hair look? What expression do you have on your face? Are you alone or with a friend? Take a few more moments and experience what you're feeling in this wonderful creative childhood memory. Are you happy? Playful? Free? Are you being sponta-neous and spunky? Are you laughing, dancing, singing, drawing, writing, or playing?

Or are you one of those individuals who can't recall ever being a creative child? Are you finding it difficult to be free, playful, and natural as you try to remember a childhood memory filled with freedom, play, and joy? If the answer is yes, what feelings come up for you? Are they emotions of sadness, pain, or resentment? If you were never allowed to be creative and a free child, then write about how that feels for you.

Now take your pen and start writing about the experience using first (I) present tense (am). Write with all your senses, describing the visual pic-tures you experienced as well as the feelings of freedom and creativity. Do not stop writing until you've written for twenty minutes. Do not take your pen from the page, and don't read over anything you've written until you're finished. Again, it's important for you to be free when you write and not to worry about grammar, spelling, or punctuation. And above all, don't edit or rewrite.

Remember, if you get stuck and can't think of anything else to write, then, write about feeling stuck and not being able to write. No matter what, don't stop writing until at least twenty minutes have passed. If you want to set a timer for twenty minutes you can, as long as you make sure not to stop until it goes off. Writing about this waking dream with no type of rules closes off your inner critic and enables you to access your free child and your creativity.

As you write from your free, playful child, allow yourself to experience feelings of spontaneity, curiosity, and freedom. Trust the process, and let yourself go with the flow. This allows you to be more creative, honest, and original. Be accepting toward your free, creative child as you practice the hab-it of being uninhibited when you're writing. Learn to trust yourself and your creative process and allow yourself to go into the unknown places it takes you. You'll be pleasantly surprised at how fantastic your writing will become and at the fabulous ideas that will bubble up as you write.

SHRINK WRAP-UP: UNTIL NEXT TIME

- Embrace primary and secondary creativity together.
- Accept that discipline and logic are as important to writing as your creative ideas.
- Write in your Creativity Chronicle and fill up the pages.

SESSION 3

On Your Mark, Get Set... Ooh, Look, *Family Guy's* On

What you are will show in what you do."
—*Thomas Alva Edison*

There are as many reasons for procrastination as there are writers. And there are times in every writer's life that procrastination rears its ugly head. Cleaning out the refrigerator or cleaning out the garage are two popular ways writers procrastinate. If you find yourself unable to write because of procrastination, it's important for you to understand a few of the leading causes of this problem.

The most prevalent reasons for procrastination are usually psychological and unconscious—hidden from your awareness. On the one hand, you desperately want to write; on the other, you simply don't. This causes you great pain and suffering. This internal conflict that manifests itself in procrastination may stem from different fears you have that are lurking just below the level of your awareness. The two most obvious are fear of rejection and fear of failure. These fears will unconsciously sabotage any long-term attempt you make to keep working on your writing project. They present themselves in the form of procrastination and not only prevent you from completing your writing, but stop you from fulfilling your goal. If you procrastinate, you can't write; if you don't write, you won't fail or be rejected. Not writing therefore becomes an act of self-protection. The feeling of rejection is a terrible one—nobody wants to experience it. And who wants to fail? No one. You may be protecting yourself by procrastinating, but in the long run you're hurting yourself more.

Procrastination affects your self-image in a negative way. You end up feeling shame and guilt when you don't write, and it soon becomes a vicious cycle. The more you feel shame, the more you procrastinate, and the more you don't write, the guiltier you feel. In other words, procrastination is not only unproductive, it also damages your self-esteem and your feelings of self-worth.

Procrastination may also be caused by your making writing the last priority on your list of things to do. In this way, you do everything before you write—wash the car, dry the dishes, walk the dog—and by the end of the day you have procrastinated so well that you don't have any time left for your writing. And it's really true. You've used up all of your precious time, and now you just can't write. Unfortunately, you may also feel weak and upset with yourself for not writing. In this case, you've made your writing the last item on your "to do" list, because you really wanted to avoid having to write in the first place.

Whatever your reasons, procrastination prevents you from completing your project and giving it your all. These few examples are just the tip of the iceberg in terms of why you procrastinate. Maybe none of the above reasons relates to you specifically. It's important for you to be able to identify why you aren't writing. Perhaps you have no idea why you procrastinate. You just know it fells terrible and that you feel guilty about not working.

In this case, one way to overcome procrastination is to enter therapy and explore your unconscious. Through self-exploration, therapy helps you bring your unconscious material into your consciousness. In the process, you discover reasons why you procrastinate, and with self-knowledge you'll hopefully begin to overcome those barriers. You can't change something you're not aware of, so the first thing to do is discover your reasons for not writing. Become aware.

First, start to question the reasons you have for not writing. You may be afraid that you won't succeed. You may think you don't really have any talent.

Or perhaps you believe you'll be rejected and you really hate rejection in any and all aspects of your life. If you continue to explore your reasons for not writing, you'll eventually bring to your awareness the truth about why you procrastinate. Remember, you can't change anything in your life or in your writing if you aren't aware of the problem. Awareness is the first step towards change.

One way to become aware of why you procrastinate is to write daily about how you feel when you don't write. Another way to be aware of your motives is to start to monitor your thoughts when you want to write but don't. Learn to be accountable for your actions or lack of actions by questioning your motive.

It's likely that you'll actually enjoy the writing process once you get into the rhythm of it. Maybe you'll begin to look forward to writing, rather than dreading it, as you become aware of what's stopping you. Moreover, your writing will most likely improve as you continue to write instead of procrastinate. Writing is a contact sport and as such needs practice, practice, and more practice. So show up, sit down, and practice.

On the Couch

"There is no agony like bearing an untold story inside of you."
—MAYA ANGELOU

Sema came to her first appointment harried and upset. She was a children's writer who couldn't write her latest book. "I don't know why I keep procrastinating, but I just can't make myself write this book."

"Perhaps you don't want to write it for reasons unknown to you," I said.
She looked at me in frustration.

"Why would I be here seeing you if I didn't want to write it? I've looked at all my excuses and they seem valid. In fact, I don't think they are excuses."

"Do you have a problem with self-discipline or will power?"

"No, I'm very disciplined in my life and in my work. It's only with my writing that I can't set goals and reach them. And I don't know why."

The real reasons for her procrastination were safely hidden away in her unconscious, just waiting to attack her when she least expected.

For the next couple of sessions we worked on her fears and I had her write about them. The next week she came back with the following list of fears:

I'm afraid I'm not really a good writer.
I'm fearful about being embarrassed by what I write.
I'm afraid nobody will buy this book.
I'm worried I'm not original with what I create.

The more she wrote, the deeper she delved into the reasons for her procrastination. I commented upon them.

"Your fears, which are responsible for your procrastination, are probably related to your childhood, when a parent or teacher said, 'That's not the way to do it,' or 'Can't you ever get anything right?'"

She thought about what I said for a long time. "But those criticisms happened when I was a kid. Why would they affect me now?"

"Because they have remained in your unconscious and have stopped you in your tracks when you want to write."

She was so upset that she still was affected from her past that tears flooded down her cheeks. "I can't believe that I'm still playing tapes of my inner critic, forty years later!"

"Amazing, isn't it, how the unconscious records everything that's happened to you and stores it away. In either case the outcome is the same—you procrastinate and remain safe."

"I might be safe, but I'm not happy."

"Exactly. You really aren't safe at all. It's only an illusion, especially since you want to be a writer more than anything else and you're not writing. And the shame you feel for not writing is a lot more harmful to you than just writing would be."

"True, but I'm still not sure what to do."

Off the Couch

"The bitterest tears shed over graves are for words left unsaid and deeds left undone."
—LILLIAN HELLMAN

As the weeks passed, we began slowly chipping away at Sema's reasons for procrastinating.

"Sema, ask yourself if you *really* have to clean your bedroom or organize your closets. If the answer is no, then don't procrastinate. Just go to your computer or notebook and start writing."

"It isn't as easy as that!"

"You're absolutely right. It isn't easy, but do it anyway. By writing, especially when you don't want to, you'll improve your self-confidence and reduce your feelings of anxiety. To paraphrase a famous saying, 'The journey of a thousand pages begins with the first word.'"

"I guess I just can't start that journey with the first word, but I'll try."

A couple of weeks later, Sema was writing a little, but she was not being productive enough to accomplish what she wanted to achieve. It was now time to take a behavioral approach with her.

"If you put your energy into your writing rather than into wondering why you procrastinate, you'll be able to start moving in a positive direction towards reaching your writing goal."

"How do I begin?"

"Just take a deep breath and begin writing, just like you would do anything else—by jumping in. Just start writing. Then you'll be doing it instead of thinking about why you're not. Remember to use Ballon Method Writing.™ Write so fast you don't have to think about or analyze why you don't' write. Besides, if you write, you'll have a chance to finish your book, but if you procrastinate you'll never have that opportunity."

"I'll try to write every other day," Sema said.

"It's a good idea for you to be specific and plan the hours, no let's say *minutes*, you'll write during the week. Start with five minutes for the first week.

Sema agreed to write for five minutes a day. She said, "I guess I can do anything for just five minutes at a time."

And you know what? She could and she did. She began to overcome her procrastination habit just by writing five minutes at a time.

Then she asked, "Rachel, can I write for longer than five minutes at a time?"

"Of course you can. You can increase your writing by five-or ten-minute increments any time you want."

She smiled. "I discovered that writing for just five minutes at a time was easy to handle. And I now want to go for longer periods."

"This is terrific, Sema. Do you realize you're now *asking* to write instead of not writing at all?"

Sema kept increasing her time by five-minute increments until she was writing an hour a day. She eventually completed her children's book and has regained her love of writing and her productivity, as her procrastination has abated.

Shrink Rap

"I'm too tired to write."
"I have to wax my car."
"My favorite movie is playing."
"I need to wash my hair."

Creativity Chronicle

Better far to write twaddle or anything, anything, than nothing at all."
—KATHERINE MANSFIELD

Make a to-do list at night, before you go to sleep. Put "Writing" at the top of your list, so that the first thing you do in the morning is write. This will permit you to finish your writing before you have time to procrastinate. Then you can schedule your other activities around your writing. By taking this action you will not only stop procrastinating, you'll counteract your negative feelings about yourself with positive ones. By replacing procrastination with productivity, you'll feel proud of yourself and your writing. And best of all you'll complete your writing project and be ready and prepared to go on to the next one.

SHRINK WRAP-UP: UNTIL NEXT TIME

- Write a daily to-do list and put "Writing" at the top of the list.
- Grab your pen and notebook and write down all the reasons you procrastinate.
- Remember: Your book or screenplay won't get done unless you write it.

SESSION 4

I Think I'm Feeling Sad/
Mad/Bad/Glad

"Feelings, nothing more than feelings..."
—MORRIS ALBERT, LYRICIST OF "FEELINGS"

To be an emotional writer, you need to channel your feelings through yourself, into your characters, and onto the pages of your stories. Emotion is what gives your writing heart. If you have trouble expressing your emotions, you won't be able to write with passion or feeling. Your characters will be flat and your stories shallow, because both will lack emotional depth.

In my book *Breathing Life into Your Characters*, I give writers exercises designed to bring their characters to life. But first, I have the writers do the same exercises for themselves. Why? *You can't give to your characters and stories emotions that you are afraid to feel yourself.* In other words, if you can't feel, then your writing won't have feeling. If you can't express your emotions, then your characters won't have emotions either.

It all begins with you. You need to be able to first access your own emotions in order to put them into your writing. Emotional writing is the best kind of writing. It makes your readers and viewers cry, laugh, rage, feel, and identify with your characters and stories. Emotional writing allows your audience to put themselves in your characters' shoes, root for and connect to them.

Trust your inner wisdom, your spirit, and your uniqueness. Your memory is a wonderful resource and repository for your heartfelt emotions. Once you've accessed those and put them on the page, they will reach your audience.

It's my belief that one of the biggest problems for writers of all genres is their inability to release their emotions. To feel is to risk. To feel is to be courageous in your writing. Unless you are connected to your emotions, you are doing nothing more than expository writing. Your emotions are the real barometer of who you are and how you feel. Do you know how you feel at this exact minute? Or don't you have any idea what you're feeling? To be a full emotional and creative writer, you must be open to all aspects of yourself; repression of your feelings works against your emotions and makes your writing flat. Before you're free to write, you need to acknowledge your emotions. Do this by clearing out your buried anger, sadness, and pain. Allow room for your creativity to shine through your writing.

In the same way you would clear out the weeds from your garden, clear out your anger and the buried feelings inside you, so that your creativity can blossom and flower. Take a "creativity colonic"—flush out your blocked ideas and emotions, and make them accessible to yourself the minute you start writing.

On the Couch

"When a man is angry and won't admit it, he always gets angry."
—THOMAS CHANDLER HALIBURTON

Recently, a new client came to see me about her writing. Cindy was a very affable young woman in her early thirties. She was frustrated because she'd rewritten her novel numerous times and still was unable to get any emotional depth into her characters. Several agents, all of whom had rejected her manuscript, had told her that her writing was static and unemotional.

"My writing is so dull, and my characters are bland and boring," Cindy revealed to me. "I get so anxious about my writing that I've recently had anxiety attacks whenever I've worked on my novel."

"Do you think that your subject matter is bringing up feelings of anxiety?"

"No, it's more about my anxiety over whether my writing is good or not, because it's not going anywhere."

After I read part of her novel it was obvious that all her characters sounded the same. "Do you realize that there aren't any emotions coming through your characters or connecting to your writing?"

"I try, but I just can't put any emotions into my story. I know my characters all sound clichéd and stilted."

"Cindy, if you aren't able to be introspective and reach inside, your writing won't have the emotional depth, because of your inability to access your feelings."

As we continued to explore the anxiety she felt when she wrote and her inability to express her emotions in her writing, we put the novel aside and discussed her childhood.

"As a child, were you allowed to express your feelings, such as anger?" I asked.

"No, I was never permitted to get angry. For that matter, I wasn't able to express any negative emotions like sadness, either. Only my parents were allowed to get angry or fight."

"No wonder it's difficult for you to put feelings into your writing, you have actually learned how to block them."

She admitted that was the case and confessed most of the time, she had no idea of what she was feeling.

"Cindy, I want you to pick an emotion from the basic ones I'm going to give you—like sad, bad, mad, or glad. I've referred to them in my book on writing lifelike characters as 'Emotions 101.' Write about a childhood memory dealing with one of these emotions—sad, bad, mad, or glad—and bring it back with you so we can discuss what you wrote in the next session."

Off the Couch

"Be happy. It's one way of being wise."
—COLETTE

When Cindy returned the following week she said, "I hadn't realized before now how all my life I've had to swallow my feelings."

She had written about a time when she was mad and how she was punished for showing her anger. This is what she wrote.

"My mother is yelling at me again. She always yells when she drinks. I wish my father would come home soon, so I can escape her anger. I hate coming home after school and wish I could be playing at a friend's. Every afternoon when I get home I can smell the liquor on her breath. She's always angry at me. Today I don't even know what I did that made her so angry. But she's glaring at me with rage as she shouts, 'You're nothing but a trouble maker. I wish I never had any kids.'

I can't take it anymore and I begin to cry. She rushes toward me and my heart flutters, with hope and I think, she's going to tell me she's sorry for yelling and wishing I weren't alive. But when she reaches me instead of hugging me she slaps me hard across my face. She hits me with so much force I fall backwards and knock over a vase, which crashes to the floor in hundreds of pieces. 'You want to cry, well, I'll give you something to cry about,' and she hits me again. I try to hold back the tears as she uses a singsong voice and says, 'What a crybaby you are. Stop it this minute you're giving me a headache. Go to your room and just wait until your father gets home.'

As I slowly walk away she shouts, 'Are you still crying?' I shake my head no as I hold back my tears. I rush to my room and can't even cry in the supposed safety of its four walls for fear she'll burst into my bedroom and yell some more. My tears are locked inside along with my broken heart. That night my father comes home and yells at me for breaking his favorite vase. I just look down and don't say a word. He takes my allowance away until I'm able to pay for buying another vase. I never tell him about my mother hitting me and knocking me down. It wouldn't matter. Nothing changes. I don't ever feel anything after that. I never shed another tear."

After listening to her read what she'd written, it was clear why she wasn't able to connect to her feelings.

"It's understandable that you're unable to write from an emotional place because you got punished for showing your feelings. But now you need to delve into your feelings and release them, so you'll feel freer and less restricted in exposing your emotions."

"It's true. Since I've been writing about my emotions I'm not as anxious as I had been."

"Good, because in order to write with power, you need to get in touch with all of your own emotions. That way you'll know how you feel, not only in your writing but in your life."

Cindy realized that in the past she always played it safe in her writing as well as in her life. We worked on the emotions she'd repressed and I had her continue to write about these different emotions. During each session she came in with her assignment and was shocked about the emotional experiences she had forgotten in her childhood. In her work and by using Ballon Method Writing,™ she was able to recall them.

"I realize now doing all this writing work that I've always swallowed my feelings and never expressed what I truly felt."

"That's because you didn't allow yourself to feel in your life, so how could you feel in your writing?"

"I now see how I've always gotten my cues from others about how I should feel. No wonder I couldn't write with emotional power."

The writing exercises she continued to do allowed her the opportunity to express feelings she had been afraid to feel.

"When I write, I can be me, and I'm now able to accept my emotions and not deny them, because of being afraid others won't approve. This is such a freeing process—to *feel*."

Cindy's anxiety attacks completely disappeared as she dug up her painful memories and dealt with them in her writing.

The last time she saw me, she said, "I feel as light as a bird and as light as the air. I realize now I'll never give up this floodgate of feelings I've released. Thanks so much for helping me find my true self and my emotional voice."

Shrink Rap

I think I'm feeling Bad, Sad, Mad, Glad—or maybe I feel Sad, Glad, Mad, Bad. Or do I feel Mad, Sad, Glad, Bad? Perhaps I'm feeling Glad, Bad, Sad, Mad.

Creativity Chronicle

"The joy that isn't shared dies young."
—ANNE SEXTON

Using Ballon Method Writing,™ write about a time in childhood or the recent past when you felt bad, sad, mad, or glad. This will enable you to liberate repressed emotions and put them into your writing.

SHRINK WRAP-UP: UNTIL NEXT TIME

- Don't be afraid of your feelings. Just feel them and you'll feel alive.
- Release your feelings into your characters and in your writing to create characters that are multi-dimensional and writing that is evocative and emotional.
- Your feelings are the true barometer of who you really are. Express them in your creativity and be an authentic human being.

SESSION 5

They Hate Me, They Really, Really Hate Me

"To conquer fear is the beginning of wisdom."
—BERTRAND RUSSELL

D o you become insecure as a writer when your writing is rejected, or if your producer doesn't like your script? Is your ego tied up with your writing, or can you separate yourself from your writing? If you fall into the first camp, you're not alone. Many writers suffer from feelings of insecurity at one time or another during their writing career. So if you feel self-doubt about your writing ability, you're not alone. Just keep in mind that your insecurity will stand in the way of your success if you don't do something about it.

Even though they might reject what you write, people really don't hate you. That's the first and most important lesson: You must separate yourself from your writing. You can be a great person but a mediocre writer, or vice versa. The good news is that you can transform your negative feelings of self-worth about your writing. It's you, and not anyone else, who has the power to improve your writing so that you'll feel more confident and competent about yourself as a writer.

Fear of rejection, fear of being incompetent, fear of taking a risk, and lack of belief in yourself are based on your perceptions and your attitudes.

You need to learn how not to worry about whether other people like your writing. Do *you* like your writing? Do you have faith in what you're writing? Keep your facts and feelings separate by learning how to be objective. One way to be objective about your writing is to put it away for a couple of weeks and then take it out and try to read it with the eye of a professional writer. You need to work on reframing your negative self-perceptions so they don't immobilize you. Make overcoming your insecurities a challenge rather than a death sentence that stops you from writing.

Lack of confidence and self-esteem are more powerful than anything else that keeps you doubting yourself. If you anticipate rejection in advance in your personal or professional life, you are creating a self-fulfilling prophecy that cannot do anything else but come true. This type of thinking will keep you stuck in your writing and will block your creativity.

If you want to be a serious writer, you need to know that rejection is part of the writing process. Even if you're rejected, don't reject yourself. You need inner strength and a belief in yourself and in your writing to succeed. Expect rejection. Accept it, and keep on writing after you get rejected. Most importantly, maintain your self-worth and your self-confidence based on who you are, not on how you write.

On the Couch

"We are our own devils; we drive ourselves out of our Edens."
—GOETHE

Lisa was raised in a family with a passive father and a critical mother who lived vicariously through her talented daughter. Although her mother was proud of Lisa's accomplishments and her writing ability, Lisa also experienced her mother's jealousy. Taking on as her responsibility, her mother's need to live through her, Lisa faced tremendous internal pressure to live not only her own life but her mother's as well. Her inner self told her to set goals and reach them, but unconsciously knew never to make her mother jealous.

Lisa's problem was that she'd met a literary agent who was very interested in reading her novel; however, she couldn't finish it. She had only a few chapters left when she called for an appointment.

"I need your help to get this completed. I feel so guilty because the agent just called me again, asking when I'd be finished. I just can't write."

I read her novel and it was excellent. I told her it was well written, and the next week she cancelled her appointment.

When she returned the following week, I said, " Lisa, it seems as if you can't tolerate compliments. I'm wondering whether you cancelled your appointment, because you felt uncomfortable when I said your novel was very well written."

She looked at me in surprise. "I never thought about that. I guess I'm almost more comfortable when I'm criticized. It's something I always expect."

"Perhaps you feel like leaving therapy, because I believe in you and your ability."

She laughed. "I must admit that I was just thinking, 'Rachel's too nice and she doesn't know the real me.'"

"I could tell you weren't comfortable. Maybe that's something you learned in childhood."

"I'm always wrestling with my own self-worth. When I'm complimented in my writing I don't even connect to that."

After seeing Lisa for a while, I realized that her block stemmed from childhood criticism and fear of not pleasing others. It was important to find out who exactly influenced her.

Off the Couch

"Do something. If it works, do more of it. If it doesn't, do something else."
—Franklin D. Roosevelt

One day I told Lisa to make a note of every time her inner voice criticized her. I instructed her to write it down in her Creativity Chronicle throughout the day or night whenever she heard the critical voice berate or belittle her.

She came in with a notebook filled with things the critical voices said, such as the following:

"You can't write."
"You're just stupid."
"Why don't you realize you have no ability?"
"Look who thinks she has something to say1"

The criticisms were endless and constant.

"No wonder you're blocked," I said. "With all that criticism raining down on you, you have no creative energy left with which to write."

I could see that she was exhausted by the daily litany of critical voices. After our session, I gave Lisa an assignment to write about a childhood memory. Her instructions were to write about a time when she felt good about being creative and then how she later felt after being criticized by someone.

The following week she started to read her assignment and ended up in tears. Here is what she wrote:

"I am playing the guitar and practicing the new chords my guitar teacher gave me. I'm really just a beginner, but I feel so happy because I'm singing a folk song that's easy to play. The song is "Michael Row the Boat Ashore," and I just have to make a couple of chord changes, so I'm able to sing and play almost at the same time. I just love the guitar and how I sound. I'm feeling really good about myself as I sing at the top of my lungs. I keep playing the song over and over, just like my teacher told me to do. My mother rushes into the room. I think she's going to tell me how good I'm playing for just being a new student, but instead I look up and see an expression of anger on her face.

'How long do I have to listen to your constant mistakes while you sing? I'm getting a headache.'

I put the guitar down and cancel my guitar lesson for the next day. I tell my mother I want to stop guitar lessons altogether and she agrees. I stop singing as well. From feeling on top of the world, I end up feeling depressed and ashamed about my musical ability."

After she finished reading what she had written, she blurted out, "It's obvious it's my mother."

Finally, she recognized her low self-esteem was connected to the critical voice of her mother that she had internalized as her own. From that point on she began to change her self-perceptions, and through our work together realized that she was entitled to and deserved to be the best writer she could be without putting herself down.

Through the writing done with me in our sessions, Lisa not only discovered new insights about how she stopped herself, but she also changed her life script from self-doubting stories to stories of confidence and creativity. The happy ending of Lisa's story is that the New York agent took her on as a client after she completed her novel.

Shrink Rap

Critical Voice: You're not a writer
Creative Voice: Be quiet. You don't know the truth.
Critical Voice: I can't believe you're trying to write a novel.
Creative Voice: I am a novelist and a darn good one.

Creativity Chronicle

"What you think of yourself is much more
important than what others think of you."
—SENECA

Write about how you feel when your writing is rejected and what your attitude is about yourself as a person. Then counteract your negative feelings and perceptions with positive ones, even if you don't believe them. Write it anyway until you can *right* out your feelings of low self-worth. Remember, you are not your writing. You are a person who writes, so start believing in yourself and your creativity and keep on keeping on.

SHRINK WRAP-UP: UNTIL NEXT TIME

- Use all these traits to write and create every day:

    Commitment
    Risk
    Energy
    Action
    Truth
    Enjoyment

SESSION 6

If Only I Were Rich/Well-Connected/ Beautiful, Then I'd Be Published

"Tentative efforts lead to tentative outcomes.
Therefore give yourself fully to your endeavors."
—EPICTETUS

Playing the victim game by blaming others and saying, "It's not my fault!" encourages feelings of helplessness and hopelessness. You may even feel that playing the "If only I were_____" game keeps you safe and secure in your "comfort zone," but in reality you end up feeling frustrated, worried, and resentful.

Do you tell yourself blaming stories that enable you to pass the buck for not writing? Or do you take personal responsibility for your actions and choices? Each moment in your writing life is a choice. You can choose to write, or you can choose to think up all the reasons why you don't write. It's up to you. Ultimately, you have to be accountable for either writing or not writing.

I see the blame game played most often when couples come in for marriage counseling. The *never* say, "I've had three divorces and five failed engagements and I'm here to find out what's the matter with me." Instead, what I usually hear is something like this: "If it weren't for this other person I'm married to, we wouldn't have these problems."

Blaming statements take responsibility away from you and place the fault on others. But in reality, you're only hurting yourself by living the victim role. You're cheating yourself and keeping yourself dependent. Most of all, you're giving away your power, and your writing is going nowhere. By pointing a finger at others, you are actually pointing three fingers at yourself. Try it and see.

Blaming can get to be a bad habit, and it's one that's difficult to break. Change your "I'd write if only" excuses into "What if" possibilities in your writing. It's important that you spend time in advancing your writing rather than expending all of your creative energy into blaming and feeling ashamed. As you will see, you can change yourself from being reactive to being proactive, from blaming to exclaiming, "I can do it!"

On the Couch

"He that is good for making excuses is seldom good for anything else."
—BENJAMIN FRANKLIN

Mary was crying so hard she could barely speak as she tried to tell me why she wasn't writing. "If it weren't for my family I'd have time to write," she sobbed. "I wish I could be the prolific creative writer I once was rather than a writer who doesn't have a moment to write. I've become so blocked because of my many other commitments."

As I listened to all of her "*if only's,*" and "*if it weren't for's,*" I thought about all the energy she could have been using to write instead of making excuses.

"Yes, you do have children and a busy schedule; however, couldn't you schedule some writing time when the kids are in school?"

"That's easier said than done," she said. "I have car pools, grocery shopping, after-school activities, doctors' appointments, and never-ending lessons for the children. I just don't have any time left for myself, let alone writing."

For the next few sessions she continued to complain how desperately she wanted to write, if only she had the time. She continued to blame her family for her failure to write. I heard different versions of the same problem, which basically had nothing to do with being too busy, and everything to do with Mary.

During our sessions I learned that Mary had been a high-powered executive before she gave up her career to start a family. I knew that as a former manager she was certainly able to allot time for writing. Instead, all she could do was recount all the reasons she wasn't able to write.

Finally, I decided it was time to get her to confront herself. "Mary, do you realize you're playing the victim? By not being accountable, you're letting everyone else take the blame for your failure to write."

She immediately proceeded to defend herself. "You just don't understand how much I do."

"Yes, I know you're busy and a conscientious wife and mother, but you are blaming your family for not writing and you need to stop doing that. It only makes you feel guilty and ashamed. Maybe you're even feeling angry at your family."

She waited a moment and finally admitted, "You're right. I do feel ashamed and even resentful, so I blame them."

"You'd feel much better about yourself and not resent your family if you made writing a part of your life. Certainly you can make it a priority on your to-do list. Think about how you can insert some time to write in your busy schedule."

"I think I can manage fifteen minutes every day."

"Don't try to write every day, just make fifteen minutes available three times a week. That's all you have to do. Does that sound reasonable to you?"

"Not every day?" she sounded disappointed.

"No, just three times a week at the most."

"Okay, I'll do it."

Off the Couch

"To travel hopefully is a better thing than to arrive."
—Robert Louis Stevenson

The following week, Mary returned with a smile on her face. Her strained look and sad expression were gone. "I did it. I wrote on three separate days for the first time in years. And I did it for more than fifteen minutes."

"Good for you," I said. "Tell me how the writing went."

"I started with fifteen minutes. I was afraid I wasn't going to be able to last that long, but the next time I looked at my watch an hour had passed. It was amazing. Once I got into the rhythm of the writing, I just kept going."

"Great."

The shame that she had felt was gone, replaced by the pride she was feeling, and the difference showed on her face. She had accomplished her goal and didn't have to expend all of her energy on blaming others. Each week her confidence grew, as she continued to write consistently for much longer periods than fifteen minutes.

"I can now see how I betrayed myself by blaming others for my lack of courage to write. I guess that I feared my writing was just too limited. So it was easier to blame my family, but now I know it was my fault. I feel so happy that I'm taking charge and writing again."

The biggest accomplishment that Mary made during therapy was not only about writing. She was finally able to be honest with herself and stop making others responsible for her failures, writing and otherwise. Mary went on to complete three short stories by being consistent in her writing. As an added benefit, as she got into the habit of writing she stopped the habit of blaming others. Her creativity overflowed into her life, and she had more energy for her family as well.

Shrink Rap

Let go of the blame game and go **FAR** *in your writing—***F***ocused,* **A***ccountable, and* **R***esponsible.*

Creativity Chronicle

"Creative ability and personal responsibility are strongest when the mind is free."
—UNKNOWN

Take a few minutes to think about all the blaming you do and how that holds you back in your writing and in your life. As fast as you can, write down the following internal dialogues you have that keep you stuck in writing in limbo. Fill in the blanks:

"If only_____."
"I'd be writing if it weren't for_____."
"I'll write as soon as_____."
"I'll write when_____."

Did you fill up an entire page in your Creativity Chronicle? If you are able to recognize yourself making these negative statements—stop! They just hold you back from your writing goals and make you feel like a victim. Awareness is the first step towards change. Hopefully you'll be able to stop playing the blame game and start writing. Replace these victim thoughts with positive actions that you'll need to take to start writing *now*.

SHRINK WRAP-UP: UNTIL NEXT TIME

- Use "possibility thinking" to change your "if only's" into "What if's."
- Put your energy into your writing and not into blaming.
- Take personal responsibility for yourself and your writing.

SESSION 7

Are You Afraid of the Writing Wolf?

Writing is easy. All you do is stare at a blank sheet of
paper until drops of blood form on your forehead."
—GENE FOWLER

Writer's block is by far the most debilitating of the crippling situations that prevent you from writing. It is an equal opportunity problem that affects screenwriters, poets, short-story writers, novelists, and nonfiction writers. It grabs hold of experienced professionals as well as rank beginners, old and young, male and female. It doesn't discriminate, but attacks most writers at some time in their careers.

People who have never experienced writer's block tend to be dismissive of the problem. "There is no such thing as writer's block. If you really want to write, you'll just do it." Not true! I've witnessed writer's block in many clients who desperately wanted to write but couldn't. Some felt guilty; others felt angry. Still others felt panicked.

Often these were established and successful writers who felt they had lost their writing ability and were all washed up. This happened when they were too blocked to meet deadlines and worried that they might lose their jobs if they didn't turn in their scripts on time. I've witnessed writers in mental anguish and emotional turmoil due to being blocked. Their pain was so palpable that they sought my professional help to release them from the bondage of the block. Blocks do exist. If you feel pain, shame, and anxiety because you can't write, you are blocked.

I have also treated clients who are professional singers, dancers, and musicians, and all of them could still perform their art when they were depressed or stressed. This is simply not true for writers. The reason is simple. Writers draw upon the same emotional energy when they write that they experience in their lives, relationships, or careers. If a writer is experiencing such negative emotions as depression or self-doubt in real life, those emotions are likely to deplete the writer's emotional reserves, leaving nothing to write on the page.

For writers, a block is not a block is not a block. Blocks come in all shapes and sizes. They hit you when you least expect and often render you helpless. I've dealt with many writers whose presenting problem was that they were blocked. Yes, it's true they all were blocked, but throughout the years I have discovered that one block is not the same as another. Some emanate from external causes, while others originate in your psychological internal makeup. Just remember that when it comes to blocks, one size does *not* fit all.

I have worked with writers who thought they were simply suffering from writer's block, but in reality their blocks were the result of something that had little or nothing to do with writing. Instead, their blocks were due to a specific situation that had occurred in their lives that psychologically prevented them from writing. Some writers experience blocks when they're going through a divorce. Others might be blocked due to a death in the family, and some might be blocked because they're under financial and economic duress. If you're experiencing any of these various stressful problems, you may find that you can't write. You feel anxious, depressed, or nervous about what's happening in your life and are not able to concentrate on writing. You become blocked, but your block is based on your life circumstances and *not* because you're stuck in writing.

As a result of my work with so many different blocked writers, I've been able to identify different sources and origins of various types of blocks. In certain cases, I've treated writers whose enthusiasm for writing their novel, screenplay, or short story suddenly vanished, and they couldn't write. The reason might surprise you: these writers didn't know how to structure their stories or what to write next. They were blocked because of lack of knowledge of the craft of writing. This type of block is not only easy to identify, it's also easy to resolve, as you will soon see.

Some writers are blocked because of lack of experience; others are blocked because of lack of confidence. Many people believe that anyone who can write a letter qualifies as a writer. Not true. If writing were so easy, a lot of you wouldn't quit after just trying to write a short story. Do you often quit because you have no awareness of what to do after your initial idea? Do you think you're blocked, when in reality you don't have the foggiest notion of how to lay out a story? That's what happened to Lee, a former client of mine. See if you can relate to his block.

On the Couch

"Don't give up. Don't lose hope."
—CHRISTOPHER REEVE

Lee, an aspiring writer, had worked in the mailroom of a well-known talent agency. His plan was to take the mailroom route to eventual success as a writer/producer. He was an attractive and very personable young man in his late twenties with a charismatic personality. He had worked at the agency for almost a year and made a lot of valuable contacts. He really was in a great position to give his screenplay to some of the important contacts he'd made within the agency and even some contacts who were clients.

In fact, there were a few junior agents, who had told him they were willing to read his script. There was just one problem. Lee hadn't even started a script, although, he had plenty of ideas.

When Lee came to see me, he said he desperately wanted to transform his great idea into a script, but he couldn't write because he was blocked.

"You have to help me, because I can't write this script, although I keep trying. I think I have writer's block."

I began to ask him questions about his structure, his main character, his story, and his theme. Not surprisingly, it turned out he wasn't blocked at all. Instead, he had no idea what I was talking about.

"Lee, what classes or books have you read about scriptwriting? You don't seem to be familiar with story structure or character development."

He laughed. "I've never studied scriptwriting. Just read a lot of scripts and it looked easy. But ever since I started to write one, I've just been so blocked I can't write. I really need your help—right now I'm in a great place for contacts that can make things happen. You've got to help me get unblocked."

Lee was surprised when I told him that he wasn't blocked—he just didn't know the first thing about structuring his story or developing his characters.

"Lee, I can see that you have little understanding about story structure, character development, dialogue, theme, climax, or resolution. It isn't that you're really blocked; you just haven't learned the craft of screenwriting, and you don't know what to do next."

I don't think he wanted to hear that he needed to learn the craft of writing and the rules of screenwriting, which are very specific in terms of both formatting and structure.

"Writing is hard work, Lee. And it's a difficult craft that needs to be mastered. Writing a script is like building a house. You need a plan and specifications. You need to lay out a blueprint for your writing, just as you need a blueprint to build a house."

"Yeah, but I need the script now. Are you sure there isn't another way?"

"You've got to pay your dues and respect the fact that writing is as complex as learning how to play the piano or violin. You'd never assume you could give a recital, just because you played 'Chopsticks' on the piano. Well, the same is true of writing. You need to learn the craft and respect the fact that writing is a skill that must be mastered."

I have him a copy of my book, *Blueprint for Screenwriting: A Complete Writer's Guide to Story Structure and Character Development*, to read before our next session. He took it so reluctantly that I wasn't sure if he'd do the exercises in the book, or for that matter read it.

Off the Couch

"A pessimist sees the difficult in every opportunity;
an optimist sees the opportunity in every difficulty."
—SIR WINSTON CHURCHILL

A few weeks later, when Lee returned, he had a synopsis and the beginning of an outline.

"I really didn't want to hear I had to read books or go to classes, but you were right about screenwriting structure. It's really hard. I mean, I laugh when I think how I was trying to write a script and didn't know what the heck I was doing."

I was glad Lee had realized the need to learn and master his craft, rather than continue to blame his inability to write on writer's block.

"Good for you," I said. "I'm glad you now realize the importance of learning about story structure, because it's really difficult."

"I'm almost embarrassed to admit I knew nothing, now that I'm learning all the work you have to do to write. It's been a real eye-opener for me."

I looked at his synopsis and the start of his outline and gave him some feedback on what he needed to do next. To my delight, Lee was cooperative and willing to pay his dues. He worked for months with me, laying down the blueprint of his script so that his structure was solid and his characters properly motivated and believable. Lee knew that he didn't want to blow his opportunity to show his contacts a great script. He recognized that he really only had one chance for his script to grab an agent or executive's interest.

Lee completed a well-structured, solid script that he was proud of and that got the interest of contacts. Who knows what will happen, but at least he did his part—he wrote the best script he could. He overcame his writing block as he learned how to master the necessary skills he needed to be a proficient writer.

If you think you're blocked in your writing, and you've never taken a writing course or read writing books, you're not blocked—you're just in the dark. You need to do the hard work that goes into writing a book, script, or play. Writing is wonderful, but it's also challenging. Be prepared for the challenge before you plunge into your writing project. It's necessary to master your craft as it is in any creative venue.

In addition to not knowing your craft, you may discover that you developed your block for protection or distraction from your true feelings. But a block doesn't protect you when it prevents you from doing that which you really love to do—write. The feeling of safety is an illusion. You can push through your block and just write until you break free of it and release your creativity. Just like this.

Shrink Rap

Me: *"I hate being blocked. I feel frustrated and weak and I want to write."*

Block: *"What are you complaining about? I'm here to help you so you won't fail."*

Me: *"You're not helping me. You're keeping me from doing what I love best."*

Block: *"I'm protecting you from getting rejected. Don't you get it? I'll keep you safe."*

Creativity Chronicle

"You gain strength, courage and confidence by every experience in which you really stop to look fear in the face."
—ELEANOR ROOSEVELT

Use the Ballon Method Writing™ to write about your block. Dialogue with your block and tell your block how you feel about it. Then become the block and dialogue with yourself. Keep on writing a dialogue with your block until you begin to free yourself from it and take away its power. Remember to write as fast as you can for at least twenty minutes, and don't read over what you've written until you've completed the exercise—or you may become blocked!

SHRINK WRAP-UP: UNTIL NEXT TIME

- Identify what kind of block you have.
- Think about the origin of your block to find its source.
- Decide if your block protects you and investigate what it protects you from.

SESSION 8

I'm Not a Real Writer, Artist, Actor

"We must have perseverance and above all confidence in ourselves."
—MARIE CURIE

It saddens me when I see talented writers who don't take themselves seriously and are afraid to write anything. They could be selling their writing, but since they don't take themselves seriously, nobody else does.

Are you a writer who takes your writing seriously? Are you committed to your writing? If the answer is no, then you must learn to be serious about your writing. Otherwise, nothing you write, no matter how great, will ever be good enough for you.

But it really all starts with your attitude toward yourself. Do you take yourself seriously as a person? Do you take yourself seriously as a writer? If you don't take yourself seriously as a human being, how will you take yourself seriously as a writer? Nobody else will if you don't.

Not taking yourself seriously in writing, as in life, is a great way to protect you from criticism, failure, and rejection. You're beating the other person to it by telling yourself you're not a serious person or writer. "Well, it doesn't matter since I'm not a real writer anyway."

You may think this is a great way for self-protection and to keep from blaming yourself or feeling ashamed. But you couldn't be more wrong. By not taking yourself seriously, you are showing lack of confidence in yourself and in what you do, whether it's in your career, in your relationships, or in your writing life. In fact, you are not only being disrespectful to your writing but to yourself as well.

Are you acting irresponsible because you don't want to be accountable for your writing? Is it easier to not take yourself seriously so you can't be hurt if nobody likes your writing? If you believe this, then you're selling yourself a bill of goods that you're not a real writer. It is just another way to not be a serious player in the writing game.

The more you don't respect yourself as a writer, the more you increase your doubt, despair and depression. These are the 3 Ds, which are enemies of your creativity. They cause your creativity to decrease, while these negative situations increase within you. These mental attitudes can deplete your energy, close off your creativity, and stifle your writing. It takes hard work and courage to stop them from overtaking you and even stopping you from writing altogether.

So what do you do? Well, you need to start respecting yourself and your writing. You do this by asking yourself how much you want to be a writer. If, in your secret heart of hearts, you really want to be a creative writer, then you need to admit it to yourself. Stand up and be counted.

Shout it loud and clear: "I really do want to be a writer and take myself seriously, as one who can achieve goals and realize my writing dreams."

If your writing gets rejected, you need to become a serious writer and make the necessary changes in your writing so that it just keeps getting better. You also need to make realistic choices that help you with your own attitude about your writing and yourself.

Don't shortchange yourself or sell yourself short as a writer. The first time you write, it doesn't have to be right; just write it. And remember that writing is a contact sport. The more you write, the better writer you'll become.

Respect yourself and your writing enough to be truthful about how you feel. Get business cards printed up with your name and, in the middle of the card, put the word "Writer" in big, bold letters. And when you pass out your card to others, just smile and believe, "I'm a writer."

Jump into the middle of your writing life and all it encompasses with courage, creativity, and commitment. Your creativity needs to be nurtured, encouraged, and given room to grow and flourish with all your wonderful ideas, inspirations, and fantasies. Be certain to make time for it to thrive. Allow yourself to have creative time *alone* so you can be *all one*—providing yourself with solitude for your creativity and your dreams.

On the Couch

"You can't go around saying you're a writer if no one will take you seriously."
—WILLIAM KENNEDY

Burt, a retired man in his middle fifties, came to see me because he had found himself blocked in his writing while working on a book of short stories. He was depressed, because he couldn't find his passion.

I asked him what he thought his passion was and gave him an assignment to write about it during our session. He tried to write, but couldn't. He was completely resistant.

"Okay, what were you experiencing as you tried to write?" I asked.

"I was just afraid I wouldn't write it well and I'd disappoint you."

"You won't disappoint me, because I'm not judging you."

"Well, maybe I'd be embarrassed in front of you," he said.

We spoke at length, and he told me that when he was in school, writing was hard work and he felt he wasn't any good at it.

"I always come from another point of view in my writing. When I write, I shut off from myself and become someone else. Besides, I'm afraid my writing is shallow."

It was clear to me that Burt didn't believe in himself or his writing. He was trying to protect his real self from scrutiny, by not going deeper inside himself.

"Your writing is as deep as you're willing to go inside yourself."

"I try to get my story down and write it, but then I worry that it's not important enough."

I asked him to write down all of the negative feelings he had about himself not being a serious writer. He had to discover the feelings that were blocking his efforts to write, especially now that he was retired and had the time to do what he'd always wanted.

When Burt returned the following week, he had written a list of all the reasons he didn't believe he was a good writer. Here is some of what he wrote:

I'm not a writer. I'm an employee.
I've never been creative in all of my life.
How can I start now that I'm too old?
I should get a part-time job and forget about writing.

After he read his list of reasons, we discussed how difficult it was for him to write when he didn't think he was good enough.

Off the Couch

"Courage is like love; it must have hope for nourishment."
—Napoleon Bonaparte

I realized that Burt was so insecure about himself as a writer that I needed to write something with him. Together, we might have a chance of breaking the ice.

"We're going to write a poem together," I said.

He looked at me, terrified. "Oh, I'm not a writer, let alone a poet. I've never written poetry.

"Don't worry; it's just an exercise, not a writing assignment. You don't have to perform. Just have fun doing this exercise. I'll write the first two lines. You read what I've written, and then you write the second two," I said.

I handed the paper to him after I wrote the following lines:

"The sky is streaked with white and pink clouds.
They almost look good enough to eat, just like the taste of cotton candy."

He hesitated and wasn't going to write, but I insisted.

"Burt, it doesn't matter what you write. This is not about being good or bad. It's not about being right or wrong. I just want you to have a little fun with this poem. Forget about yourself and just write anything. It doesn't have to make sense or even rhyme."

At first, he could barely write, but at my urging he finally wrote and with great effort he added two more lines:

"I remember going to the carnival in town and rode the merry-go-round, round and round.

Maybe it was the carnival or maybe it was a high-school trip to Magic Mountain?"

Okay, so you get the idea. As he wrote our joint poem, I observed as he labored with the writing. After we finished I had him read the poem—twice.

"Did you discover anything about yourself?" I asked.

"Not really."

"Well, I did! Every line you wrote was a question, like this: "I wonder if I need limits?' after I had written about 'The sky's the limit!'"

As he looked over the poem, he realized how he analyzed everything about himself.

"It's no wonder you can't write, since all you did was question your ability and yourself. I wonder if you even believe you have any right to write."

I continued to point out how cautious he was and how his insecurity about his writing kept him from having any enjoyment.

"You can change this. We're going to write something together next session, and this time I want you to concentrate on having pleasure with the words and not on questioning yourself."

He returned for the following session more relaxed, now that he realized he didn't have to prove himself anymore.

"Burt, just write and be into your writing, and enjoy the process. You'll become a writer through letting go and being in the flow."

"You're right. I know that I'm too intense and I don't have any fun as a writer."

For his final assignment, I asked him to write about just that. Here's the essay Burt wrote, titled It's Time to Take Myself Seriously as a Writer.

"That has always been hard for me to do. How can I take my writing seriously, when I've never really taken myself seriously? But it's now time to do so, because I want to be a serious writer. I have ideas and beliefs that I want to share with others. It's especially important for me to share my views of the world through writing.

When I was younger, nobody in my family ever took me seriously. My role was to be the one who made my unhappy family laugh. I could deflect their pain and unhappiness if I could make them laugh. I was the prankster at home and then became the class clown in school. Those roles served me well. I made my friends laugh and that way they couldn't see my sadness inside. They didn't see me, and nobody ever took me seriously. In fact, I didn't take myself seriously either.

But through my writing and my therapy, I've learned I'm more than I seem on the outside and as perceived by others. I'm now able to have original thoughts and see myself as I really am through the words and sentences and pages I write. I have a lot to say and I want to take my writing seriously, so I can succeed in doing something I love to do. It's time to take myself seriously in order to survive and live my life on the page."

Burt eventually got in touch with the writer within and stopped writing from his critical self. He also now takes himself seriously as a writer and enjoys the writing.

Shrink Rap

Play with the words on the page, as you let them fall from your fingertips like raindrops fall onto the earth.

Creativity Chronicle

"Be good yourself, and the world will be good."
—HINDU PROVERB

Write for twenty minutes on the subject "It's time to Take Myself Seriously as a Writer." Remember to use the Ballon Method Writing.™

SHRINK WRAP-UP: UNTIL NEXT TIME

- Remember to respect yourself as a writer, but first as a person.
- Take yourself seriously as a writer, but not too seriously.
- Your self-perception will define your writing ability.

I Have Nothing to Say

"Words, words, mere words, no matter from the heart."
—SHAKESPEARE

The logo for my business (see *www.rachelballon.com*) shows a pen as part of a heart, which is the only way I believe you need to write. What is there to write if it doesn't come from your heart? I've helped thousands of writers—privately and in my "Writing from the Heart" workshops—learn how to dig inside to find their buried treasures. Writing from the heart creates the story beats, which come from their beating hearts.

Everybody has a story to write. Writing stories without heart is like marrying without love. And the results for both are the same—they go flat and don't last.

Everything you'll ever need to write for the rest of your life is already inside you. Your dreams, your childhood, your hopes, your life experiences, your fantasies, and most of all your timeless memories are the richest sources for your stories from the heart.

As long as you're alive and living your life, you will always have something to write. It's true. Just think about how some of the most famous writers made their living by writing from their life. Neil Simon and Woody Allen are two contemporary writers who have written novels, screenplays, and plays about themselves, their psyches, and their lives. Eugene O'Neill and Tennessee Williams wrote plays and prose about their tragic lives.

For those of you who now plan to write about your lives, please don't write directly about your latest family feud or your broken-hearted love affair. No, that would be boring to everyone. What you need to learn in order to be a creative writer is to take an aspect of your life that is an emotional experience or a high peak experience and transform it into fiction. Don't rush to send your diary or journal to a publisher, producer, or editor—it won't sell. What sells is writing from the heart. To write from the heart is to take a memory or a personal experience and then put it into a fictional story with memorable characters and to express your heartfelt emotions in that story.

I always say, "If you write from your heart, you'll give your stories heart and touch the heart of others. Your creative ideas, which you put into your writing, come from your humanity and they are universal. The ultimate obligation you have as a writer is to write your truth and to entertain your readers and viewers with a professional, well-crafted story from the heart."

Do you say things like this to yourself?

"I have nothing to write about."
"It's been said better by other writers."
"I have nothing earth-shattering to write."
"My life is boring."

These thoughts come from your limited thinking. Limited thinking keeps you from succeeding in your writing and in your life. Limited thinking stops you before you even get started. These self-limiting thoughts end up crippling your creativity and imagination. Don't believe them. You have a repository of stories that are meaningful and emotional, if only you don't discount them.

Don't avoid looking inside yourself. If you do, you'll lose parts of yourself, and you won't be able to put those rich feeling into your writing. This will prevent you from becoming an emotional writer and reconnecting to your inner self.

It is important for you to recognize and respect your creative imagination and your wealth of memories, for they are a gold mine for your stories. So start digging inside your heart and soul to mine the gold within.

On the Couch

"We are what we accept ourselves as being.
We can be what we convince ourselves we can be."
—*ELMER G. LETERMAN*

Jack came to see me in a panic. I had taught screenwriting at his film school, and he came to see me because he had to turn in a synopsis of his script in order to get his short film approved.

"I don't have any idea of what I'm going to write and it was due last week, but I got an extension."

He told me some of his ideas, but they all were just action-oriented with almost no story.

"The problem you're having is that you're looking outside yourself for material rather than writing from the inside out."

"But I can't think of anything in my life that is exciting to write about," Jack said. "And I need something in the next few days or I won't graduate."

I asked him about situations in his childhood that he could write about, since childhood is such a fertile and creative place from which to write.

"You have to start tapping into your most creative resource—your inner self—for the material you need. Forget the special effects and the action-packed ideas. Get in touch with an emotional memory or a memory from your life that was a peak moment."

"But that's not artistic or creative," he protested.

"Jack, a powerful script comes from reaching inside and writing the small personal story from your heart."

Jack returned and at first wasn't able to reach inside himself. "I've thought of a couple of childhood incidences, but I think they're boring. Who wants to hear about me?"

He resisted and I persisted. I told him that those very stories that he thought were dull and commonplace were, in reality, exciting and interesting.

"Don't you realize that the stories that touch the heart are the only stories that have meaning to yourself as well as to your audience? You're trying to write a script filled with special effect and bombs bursting all over the place and not about the humanity of your life."

Jack still wanted to write something splashy, edgy. "I just don't think my life is very special or, for that matter, of importance."

I told him to reconnect to some powerful memories and write from his life so that he could transform them into a short film.

"Trust me about this, Jack. Write a script that has heart and soul. If you only concentrate on context rather than content, it won't matter, because it's not about your passion, your vision, and your spirit. Next time I see you, I want to hear about some emotional experiences in your life that had meaning for you."

Jack left the session unhappy with my insistence that he reach inside himself to find the real gem of his story.

Off the Couch

"One should never write down or up to people, but out of yourself."
—CHRISTOPHER ISHERWOOD

When we met for the next session, I was amazed. Jack had not only written some ideas, he had begun the rough draft of a synopsis for his short film script. He could hardly contain his excitement.

"I can't believe what happened. After I got home, I started to think about my childhood just like you said to do. And I remembered some really interesting and meaningful experiences that I hadn't even considered before I came to see you. I wrote about a time when a school bully who had always picked on me followed me home and started his usual taunting and name-calling. I remember that I suddenly flipped out and turned around and punched him in the face. I not only surprised him, I surprised myself, and he never bothered me again."

"That sounds like a moment of truth, your moment of courage. How did you feel about that incident?"

"I felt great. It was a life-changing action for me. I realized that I wasn't the little frightened kid anymore, but that I could stand up for myself. Anyhow, once I recalled the situation, I couldn't stop writing."

It was obvious that when Jack got back in touch with his life, he began to mine the real buried treasures that resided inside him—his emotional life experiences.

"It seems your writer's block has disappeared."

"Not only has it left me, but I've already sketched out an idea for another script I'm going to write after I shoot my short film."

The story Jack needed was already written inside him—his memories. His idea for his short film was terrific, and he worked diligently to also make it a well-structured piece. As he tapped into his memories, he was able to free up his creative imagination and use his life as a jumping-off point to leap into his creativity and write from the heart.

His script was approved for his short film and he graduated with his class. He even entered his film into the short film category at film festivals nationwide and won several awards for it.

Shrink Rap

Write from your heart and you'll say what's true. Write from your heart and you'll touch mine, too.

Creativity Chronicle

"Fine art is that in which the hand, the head, and the heart go together."
—*JOHN RUSKIN*

Write about some meaningful heartfelt memory from your past. As you write, be in the moment, and write from the heart so that you can touch the heart of others.

SHRINK WRAP-UP: UNTIL NEXT TIME

- Look inside yourself and write from your heart.
- Stop your limited thinking so your unlimited creativity is available to you.
- Learn to turn your memories into powerful writing pieces.

SESSION 10

I should Be Running Paramount/ Random House/Earth

"And never hope more than you work."
—Rita Mae Brown

Unrealistic expectations always lead to disappointment. I've met writers who say, "People will steal my ideas, so I don't want to discuss my writing in front of other people." Face reality. Nobody wants to steal your ideas—other writers have a difficult enough time developing their own ideas.

Over the years, I've heard some wildly unrealistic expectations from writers who consulted with me, enrolled in my workshops, or read my previous books. Recently, I received an e-mail from someone who wanted to send his ideas, which he said were terrific, to the networks and asked me how to find their addresses. I wrote back and told him not to bother to send his ideas to the networks; they wanted completed scripts or teleplays and wouldn't even look at any unsolicited materials.

He e-mailed back and was quite upset. "These are fabulous ideas, so why wouldn't they want them?"

It was obvious that he had unrealistic expectations not only about his ideas, but also about the inner workings of the entertainment industry.

Another individual came to see me and asked if I'd write a script from his idea. I told him I had too many of my own ideas that I didn't have time for. "If it's your idea, you are the best person to write it," I said.

"No, if you won't write it, I'm going to pay someone else to write my idea and send it to the studios, and when they buy it, they can pay someone else to write it."

Just another unrealistic expectation.

I consulted with a student in one of my workshops who had refused to discuss her novel in class for fear that someone would steal it. No amount of trying to convince her that everybody was involved in his or her own story would dissuade her. She eventually came to see me as a client so that she could discuss her story privately.

Another writer in one of my workshops was worried about getting cheated out of the foreign distribution rights for a script, he hadn't as yet written. A writer working on her novel was so worried about how she'd look for her book tour that she decided to begin dieting even though her novel hadn't even been published.

This would all be humorous if the people involved weren't so tied into believing their own unrealistic expectations. In my classes there are always those writers who talk about how they're going to be selective in choosing the publishing company or studio after they get a bidding war going for either their script or novel. This is more than an unrealistic expectation; it's rather grandiose thinking.

Most of these unrealistic expectations arise out of ignorance of writing itself and the writing world. My suggestion to anyone who wants to write for a particular genre is that you know the market for which you want to write. Study it and learn all its ins and outs so that you don't waste your time or anyone else's with unrealistic expectations. It's a sure sign of being an amateur, when you don't even know the players or how to be a player in the writing game. Your unrealistic expectations will block your creativity and prevent you from ever realizing your writing dreams.

Writing is a business, and as such, you need to be intelligent and savvy about it. Know the market for which you want to publish or produce, and study it like you would any other subject in which you want to be knowledgeable.

Do your research and learn the names of agents, producers, editors, managers, and magazine editors. There is nothing worse than sending a query letter to an editor or producer who is no longer working at the company. Use resources like the *Creative Directory* or Writer's Digest marketplace books to help you find this information. They'll give you the names of the people in charge and the type of scripts or manuscripts they're looking to buy. You wouldn't send a nonfiction book on gardening in Asia to Bantam Books. Nor would you submit a low-budget independent script to Warner Brothers.

When you send out material be smart, be sharp, and be realistic.

Making an assumption that is larger than reality sets you up for bigger disappointments. Do you know why you have such unrealistic expectations? There could be many reasons. Maybe you have developed a distorted view of yourself to cover up feelings of low self-esteem. Maybe you're protecting your feelings of insecurity or inferiority. Maybe you really believe your grand plans and great expectations. Or maybe you suffer from feelings of grandiosity about your writing ability and overestimate yourself.

Well, whatever the reasons, you need to take a reality check and see how much you're hurting yourself by not being realistic. Are you stopping yourself from achieving your writing goals because of your huge expectations? Or are you unconsciously setting yourself up for disappointment and making your writing career the scapegoat for all of your other unrealistic plans that didn't come to fruition?

You will succeed with your writing if you set realistic goals and take the necessary steps to get informed, not only about the genre in which you write, but also about the submissions, the proper format, and researching the companies where you plan to send your final writing project. Be prepared, be real, and write.

On the Couch

*"Don't bother just to be better than your contemporaries
or predecessors. Try to be better than yourself."*
—WILLIAM FAULKNER

"I was so ambitious I passed myself up," said Bob, a handsome actor who became a screenwriter.

"I was so into getting ahead of my reality as a screenwriter that now I can't be myself and don't know how to write what I want, because for so long I've been running away from who I really am."

"What do you mean by 'running away from who you are?'"

"Listen, I have a mask like everyone else in this business, so I act confident and cool, but inside I'm scared I won't sell another script."

Bob had acted for years before he wrote a low-budget screenplay and starred in the movie. Since then he had written a couple of spec scripts, hoping to find a home for them with a production company or a studio, but with no luck.

The problem with nobody buying his scripts was that he had given up his acting and now made his living as a professional writer. Therefore, when he didn't sell his scripts, he faced serious financial problems. He needed help in sorting out his writing life.

"I got so used to writing to please others that I no longer feel my own vision or have any idea what to write that will sell."

"You certainly have a lot of expectations of yourself. After all, not everything you write *will* sell."

He kept on talking, as if to himself, because he was feeling so anxious and disappointed.

"I constantly have to go out and pitch my ideas to other people in the business, and lately I feel so hopeless."

"What's going on?" I asked.

"I'm writing to please everybody, least of all myself. And I'm trying to second-guess what they want, so I've lost my original voice and my reason for writing. In the beginning, before I knew how crazy this business was, I wrote meaningful scripts. The first was a small-budget movie, but it was made."

"That's because you were passionate about it."

"You're right. I thought that it would be easy street from there on in and had great expectations for my other scripts. I think they were realistic, but I 'm not sure anymore. Anyhow, the more scripts I write, the less hope I have, and more disappointments have followed."

"It's a tough business," I added.

"Yes, and now I'm depressed because I try to guess what the networks and studios want, and I'm totally confused by the whole process. At first they're excited, and then the next thing I know they give me tons of notes and want me to start rewriting everything that they had originally liked—for no money. And right now I need money to pay the rent and buy food—little things like that.

"When you write with tons of expectations of what you want to happen to your writing, this will certainly prevent you from being creatively free and enjoying the writing process. I'd like you to make a list of all the expectations you have for your script before you even start to write. Let's get them out there in the open."

Off the Couch

"Everywhere in life, the true question is
not what we gain, but what we do."
—THOMAS CARLYLE

Bob returned the following week with a list of his expectations. As he read them, I could tell that some were realistic but most were not:

"I want my next script to be sold for a million dollars."
"I plan to win an Academy Award for one of my scripts."
"I want to live in Malibu and drive a Porsche."
"I want to make a three-picture deal with a major studio."

"Bob, wanting to make money and make a living as a writer is certainly realistic, because you've already done that. The problem is if you can continue doing it, since this business is so unpredictable and what was selling last year is in the slush pile this year."

"I guess you're right. This is a crazy business, where the writer is the least important person in turning a script into a film. It's all those twenty-something M.B.A.'s from Harvard who make the creative decisions."

"Don't you know that in the entertainment business the creative line has been replaced with the bottom line?"

"I guess I felt I could rise about the politics of Hollywood," he replied.

As I listened to Bob's point of view, I began to see why he was feeling so desperate, aside from the real worries about money. He was actually setting himself up for failure with his myriad unrealistic expectations.

"No wonder you don't write. With all these things at stake, the pressure you're putting on yourself is enough to stop you from ever writing. You are putting yourself in a pressure cooker and you don't need anyone else to do it."

"So what am I supposed to do? Just quit being a writer?"

"No," I said. "Just let go of your unrealistic expectations. Stay in the present. You won't have a future with your writing if you don't get into the joy of writing again and start enjoying the process rather than concentrating on the results."

'But I don't know how to stop," Bob said, desperate and upset.

"Okay, circle the expectations on your list that are reasonable and reachable and discard the unrealistic expectations, so that you are free to write without the heavy burden of the outcome."

After Bob had discarded the unrealistic expectations, he seemed more relaxed the next time we met.

"You know, I didn't realize what a burden I was putting on myself by having all these unreasonable and unrealistic expectations."

"I agree. Worrying about winning an Academy Award for your next script is unrealistic. Also, to buy a house in Malibu, you'd have to sell a lot of scripts. These are just a few of your unrealistic expectations that drag you down and lead to disappointments."

During the following session, we worked together on Bob's goals that were realistic. He set up a writing schedule so as to reach them with hard work.

After several sessions, Bob was less depressed as he came in to see me. He had written not only his goals to reach his writing expectations, he also had written twenty pages of his script.

"A couple of weeks ago, when I did the exercise about writing down all my expectations, I felt a heavy weight being lifted from my creative writing. It was like a surge of creative energy filled my body. I'm now writing my script and remembering why I wanted to be a writer in the first place. Thanks for bringing me back to reality."

Shrink Rap

How extraordinary to be so ordinary. How ordinary to be so extraordinary.

Creativity Chronicle

"Keep your eyes on the stars and your feet on the ground."
—THEODORE ROOSEVELT

Do your homework and familiarize yourself with the marketplace and the genre in which you're writing. Make a list of all of your expectations—realistic and unrealistic. Be a realist, and study the marketplace before you decide how much money you're going to make in your field. Write about setting realistic goals and taking the necessary steps you will need to reach these goals.

SHRINK WRAP-UP: UNTIL NEXT TIME

- Remember to reconnect with the joy of writing and be in the process rather than the product.
- Keep your expectations realistic so you won't be disappointed.
- Don't substitute pipe dreams for hard work. Write.

SESSION 11

It's My Mother's Fault

"No rewards are offered for finding fault."
—UNKNOWN

Not writing can be crippling to your creativity. Frustrations, tensions, and anxieties often arise when you have trouble getting started to write. The two basic direct responses to frustration are either fight for flight.

Fight is usually a destructive physical act that leads to further conflict. Flight is taking a direct action to get away from frustration, as in running away, escaping, hiding, taking off, running from problems, running from relationships, and even running from your writing.

Let's look at the some of the less obvious reactions to frustration and conflict, especially as they relate to blocks to creativity. The most common methods of flight are indirect actions, such as daydreams, fantasies, disinterest, tuning out, and apathy.

These are defenses used to reduce anxiety, repress unpleasant experiences, and prevent frustration and discomfort when facing criticism or embarrassment in your writing. They help you to keep going in the face of rejection and aid you when you become too frustrated to write. You may often resolve your conflicts with creativity. Yet, there are the more deeply rooted frustrations and conflicts that aren't resolved by fight or flight and lead to development of defense mechanisms.

Defense mechanisms are unconscious attempts to protect yourself against threats to the integrity of the ego. In the case of creativity, they help you protect yourself against threats to your writing. They also relieve tensions and anxiety resulting from unresolved frustrations. Rationalization is a common defense mechanism, in which you explain your behavior by giving it a good reason:

"Oh, I'm not writing today because it's a holiday and I need my rest."
"I know I shouldn't watch television instead of writing, but it's okay once in a while."
"I'm not writing because the computer gives me a headache."

These are rationalizations to justify your not writing. The reasons may seem logical, but they are still nothing more than excuses, and behind them are the real frustrations that actually prevent you from writing.

Projection is another defense mechanism. It works by allowing you to protect yourself by putting all the bad traits you may have on others and away from yourself. Often you can project the blame for not writing on others because it's too painful to feel that you're the one who's creating your own blocks. Projection is all about not accepting your own impulses—the ones you don't like. You then accuse another person of having those very same negative feelings you don't want to admit as your own, such as procrastination, avoidance, and rationalization for not writing. Projection helps protect you from overwhelming feelings of self-doubt and despair.

When you write, your defense mechanisms also prevent you from experiencing your anxiety and keep your emotional landscape intact. This is especially true when you're frustrated with your writing or feel conflicted because your writing keeps getting rejected.

Does your defense mechanism keep you safe from the painful feelings you experience when you aren't creative? Have defense mechanisms become such a part of your life that you use them more than you write? Do you protect yourself from put-downs by others, especially when your writing is criticized?

Well, you can't change what you aren't aware of. If you keep putting up defenses to avoid the reality of your writing frustrations, you'll never learn the truth about yourself as a writer. You certainly don't want to experience a downward spiral and get completely blocked, do you?

Even though defense mechanisms are helpful to your emotional well-being and survival, they often work against you because they keep you from dealing with issues about your writing that need to be cleared away. They basically allow you to delude yourself and prevent you from finding real solutions to your writing problems.

Defense mechanisms also keep you in situations where you're not being responsible for your writing life. For example, saying, "It's my mother's fault I'm not writing," is the same as saying "The devil made me do it."

Don't blame someone outside of yourself when in reality you're the one choosing whether or not to write. Hopefully, you can stop being defensive and start taking the offensive with your writing.

On the Couch

The less a person understands his own feelings, the more he will fall prey to them."
—HOWARD GARDNER

"Yes, but…you don't understand what I'm trying to write." Bernie was a young screenwriter in his early thirties. "I hate when other people try to force their opinions about what I should do with my script."

Bernie came to see me about his screenplay and all I heard was "Yes, but…Yes, but…Yes, but…" every time I tried to discuss his structure, characters, or plot with him. He was the most defensive writer I had ever worked with and couldn't hear any suggestions.

"I don't understand why you came to see me for a script analysis if you don't want to hear or consider any suggestions I make."

"It's just that the script is my vision and the characters are my characters and I don't want to change them."

"But it's not helping you if you take the advice so personally and become so defensive," I said.

"I just wanted your feedback, but I'll think about it."

Bernie just couldn't seem to face what he had to do as a writer who wanted to improve his script and make it saleable.

"Well, why won't the agents or the producers who've read your script take it on?"

"Those agents and producers don't know what they're talking about. My script is good and they just don't see it."

"You really are well defended. In some areas that tactic might serve you well, but you really need to be more objective where you writing is concerned. You need to rewrite your script because it's not working the way it's now written."

Bernie resented my confronting him about his writing, but after a few sessions he eventually became willing to stop being so defensive.

Off the Couch

"Don't find fault; find a remedy."
—HENRY FORD

Bernie and I kept working together on his protective defenses until he eventually was able to become less defensive and more reasonable.

"Bernie, you have to get through your defenses in order to write your truth."

"I think I'm honest in my writing."

"You are; however, you need to be willing to rewrite and be objective rather than too protective."

"I know I've always been defensive, but that's because I had to be growing up in my family."

"That's true, but once you make the internal decision to let go of your defenses you'll be a writer who writes with confidence and honesty."

It was Bernie's own resistance that kept him defensive until he began to trust me enough to feel safe and let down his guard.

"I was really angry when you told me I had to face the truth about being too defensive, Rachel. But thank you because you were right. I hope when I write my next script I'll be more open and take the advice I need to make it better."

Bernie went on to write more scripts and became a real professional who would listen to suggestions for his script and take them in order to make his script work, without the need to protect himself through all his defense mechanisms.

Shrink Rap

Stop rationalizing, projecting, avoiding, repressing,
Just face your fears and stop obsessing.

Creativity Chronicle

"What are fears but voices airy? / Whispering harm where harm is not."
—WILLIAM WORDSWORTH

Write down all the defense mechanisms you use as a writer and in your life. Are you too defensive? Do you constantly rationalize the reasons that you don't write? Write about the ways you use defense mechanisms in your writing life to protect you from frustrations or pain. Next, write how you can be a better writer by letting go of your defenses.

SHRINK WRAP-UP: UNTIL NEXT TIME

- Recognize that your own resistance is often your biggest writing problem.
- Don't be defensive when you're given good advice; get out of your own way.
- Try to identify when you project feelings about your own writing onto other writers.

SESSION 12

Ooh, Now *Modern Family* Is On!

"Clean white paper waiting under a pen is a gift
beyond history and hurt and heaven."
—JOHN GIARDI

There are many different reasons that any writer might have trouble getting started writing. Regardless of whether you're on a loose schedule or a tight deadline, you can have trouble getting started. Even if your writing is flowing and you're halfway through your screenplay, novel, or short story, you can still find yourself having trouble getting started to write.

Trouble getting started can be terrifying if your goal is to write a Pulitzer Prize-winning play or a Tony-nominated musical. Let expectations go. Just fill up the page with words, glorious words, a word at a time. Use Ballon Method Writing™ to get the words quickly down without thinking of grammar, spelling, sentence structure, or punctuation—just let the pen fly across the page.

The problem of getting started has as much to do with your knowledge or lack of knowledge of the writing process, as it does with your psychological attitude. It concerns your approach towards creativity as well as your experience with the craft.

What is your trouble with getting started? Is it a daily, weekly, monthly, or yearly struggle? If it happens all the time that you just can't write, then your trouble getting started has to do with creative blocks. If you avoid writing just some of the time, then your problem might be avoidance or procrastination. If you can't get started when you just have a few pages to write before you're done with your novel, then it might be fear of results.

Since blocks come in all different shape and sizes, it's important to discover your reason for having difficulty. They're what I call stumbling blocks to success. Each is a block in its own right, with the power to keep you from getting started. But they are also very different.

Stumbling blocks can be situational, like just having a problem with a certain aspect of your writing. Maybe one of your characters is giving you trouble, or maybe you're having difficulty with a turning point. Though they are annoying, stumbling blocks don't keep you from writing for too long. When you solve your situational writing problem, you just pick yourself up, brush yourself off, and start writing all over again.

Roadblocks usually stop you in your tracks. You can't get started because you suddenly came upon a detour or barrier to your writing that influences your creativity. The problem could have to do with your writing or with your life. Maybe you've unexpectedly lost your job or you've had a bad breakup with your mate. Or maybe you start to suspect that there's a serious flaw with your story structure, or that one of your pivotal characters is simply not believable. Whatever the problem, it stops your creativity from flowing. In this case, you need to go around your roadblock or take another path so you can continue writing.

Concrete blocks are the most difficult to overcome because they're inside you and not the result of any outside situation. You need to chip away at these concrete blocks and dig them up with your pen. They need to be pushed aside and broken into pieces through your insights, awareness, or therapy. You need to get to the source of your concrete blocks and turn them into dust.

What are the thoughts that stop you when you start writing? Do you want to be brilliant? Does your writing just have to be the best it can be right away, even as you put down your thoughts from your head to the page? Are you worried about whether you'll have anything meaningful to write? Do you want to be too literary and too pretentious?

When something constantly stops you from getting started, it often has more to do with your insides than with the writing process itself. Maybe you're too insecure, too frightened, too unsure of your writing ability, or too rigid about yourself and your work. Whatever your reasons for having trouble getting started, you can see that it's not just one block fits all.

Fighting your own resistance is one of the most difficult steps you need to take in order to write. I tell all writers that it doesn't have to be *right*, just write it.

Ask yourself where you want to be with your writing in a year or two. Do you want to have completed a body of work, or do you still want to be waiting to get started? It would be a sad situation for you if you never completed your novel/script/memoir/nonfiction book.

On the Couch

"Get black on white."
—Guy de Maupassant

Josh came to see me after he became chronically blocked in his writing. He had just completed his dissertation for his doctorate in humanities and was starting to work on his novel again. But he wasn't able to write at all and came to see me after a few months of being blocked.

At thirty-five, Josh was desperate to finish his novel now that he had some free time again. On his own, he had tried to get back into it several times, but he couldn't get anything down. He was demoralized when he came to see me.

"I'm really in a stuck place. I've been suffering from the biggest writing block I've ever had with my writing. I just can't get into my novel again."

"Tell me about it," I said.

"I've just finished my dissertation and now have time to complete my novel, but I'm not able to. I'm wasting precious days, weeks, and months of my life. I really need your help."

"What happens when you try to start your novel?"

"I just want to be the best I can be and I think about all the wonderful writers like F. Scott Fitzgerald, Saul Bellow, and Joan Didion. I guess I want to write like them. But I get into comparisons and I feel like a frustrated writer who can never reach his potential."

"It's really essential for you not to compare yourself to other writers and just get down the important things you need to write for your novel. Don't be pretentious in your writing. Just be natural."

I saw how controlling he was trying to be with his writing and I gave him a writing exercise. "Write about a time when you felt free and not restricted like you presently are feeling. You can write about a time in your childhood or from the not-too-distant past when you felt courageous."

At first he looked at me puzzled and asked, "What does this have to do with my being blocked?"

"Just do the exercise and next week you'll find out."

The following week he read what he had written about his love for skateboarding when he was a kid. This is what Josh wrote:

"Every chance I get, I run to my skateboard after school and the two of us escape together from all the things I have to do every day. On weekends I take my skateboard and we fly down the hills at the end of my street. I get a rush of freedom and excitement as I whiz by the houses and how they are nothing but a blur to me. My hair flies back and the wind on my face feels great. My skateboard leads me to new pastures and together we explore different parts of my neighborhood. We are friends. I wear a helmet, but don't feel constricted by it. I feel smart because I do fall but I don't get hurt, and I'm fearless. I just get up and jump on my board again and keep on moving. I'm trying to do some new tricks, but the best part of skateboarding is that I'm free to fly with the wind and dance in the breeze. Nothing and nobody can stop me and I let off steam, anger, and the frustrations of the day and feel better when it's time to go home and do my chores."

Josh's writing was free and natural as he described his love of skateboarding. There was no affectedness or pretentiousness in it.

"I want you to notice that when you skateboarded you didn't try to be perfect, but you just dove in and enjoyed the freedom and fun of the speed and the challenge, falls and all."

"You're right," he smiled. "I've been trying too hard with my writing and not having any fun with it."

"I want you to write with the same abandon that you skateboarded with when you were younger."

Off the Couch

What would life be if we had no courage to attempt anything?"
—VINCENT VAN GOGH

Josh returned the next week and read what he had written, which had the same feelings that his skateboarding did.

"Your writing has a completely different energy than it had before."

"I know, because I've written with the same attitude I had when I was a teenager—free and fearless."

He was so happy and couldn't wait to tell me about his process.

"I just jumped into the writing and wrote with abandonment. I noticed that my writing had a rhythm and a definite movement of speed and energy. It was great writing about those times, because it reminded me of when I felt free and would take risks."

Josh had overcome the need he had to try to be a brilliant writer. This time he just enjoyed the ride. The last session I had with Josh he told me, "I feel less cautious and more open in my writing. My energy has soared."

"Yes, the freedom in your writing allows you more freedom in your relationships and your life," I said.

"It's true. I now plunge into my writing and my life, taking risks in both. I'm having more fun in my life, and I'm more confident in my writing than I've been in the last ten years. I can't believe that this is all happening just because I jumped in and started to write throwing caution to the wind."

Shrink Rap

"I'm getting ready for getting ready for getting ready for getting ready.

Creativity Chronicle

"Faith is daring to do something regardless of the consequences."
—SHERWOOD EDDY

Start anywhere you want—in the middle, in the end, at the beginning of your story. Get your creativity revved up and let it flow, flow, flow onto the pages without thinking about it. Write about a time when you were free, took risks, and lived just in the moment. Maybe you were driving a car, running a race, riding a horse, surfing. Write with all your senses and throw caution to the wind as you describe with speed and the wonderful time you recall from your past. Keep the same energy and momentum in all of your writing, especially when you get started.

SHRINK WRAP-UP: UNTIL NEXT TIME

- Jump-start your writing and let the words flow like a river of creativity.
- It doesn't have to be right—just write it and enjoy.
- Stop trying to be unnatural with your writing and seek the freedom to play with the words on page after page after page.

SESSION 13

So, It's My 768ᵗʰ Draft and It's Almost Right

*"Be ever soft and pliable like a reed, not
hard and unbending like a cedar."*
—THE TALMUD

What is perfectionism? Perfectionism is the belief that what you write is never good enough. It is just another form of being blocked. You're unable to write anything unless it's perfect. Perfectionism keeps you from starting your writing project and prevents you from writing, in general. Fear of embarrassment and wanting to impress are usually factors in your need to be perfect.

When you're a perfectionist, you become inflexible, rigid, and controlling in your writing. Your need to be right and perfect and to keep from looking bad creates inflexibility, immobility, and rigidity inside you. Your fear of being a bad writer if you're not perfect is rooted in childhood, when you probably had parents who told you to "color inside the lines," not make any mistakes in your homework, and be a perfect little girl or boy.

If this was the case for you, then you learned that in order to get love, you had to *earn* love by doing a "perfect job" and not making mistakes.

Perfectionists are afraid of risks, and if you don't learn to take risks in your writing, you won't grow as a writer. If you try to be "right" when you start to write and try to make no mistakes, you're setting yourself up for failure. You're inhibiting your creativity. These rigid beliefs don't allow you to make a mistake, and there's no room for imperfection even in your first drafts.

You develop self-consciousness and self-importance, feeling that your writing must be brilliant and perfect or it's nothing. Guess what? There isn't such a thing as perfect. There's a saying that goes like this: "One man's meat is another man's poison." How true.

Are you a perfectionist who is afraid of taking chances, of being different, and of not looking at new creative ideas because they many not be perfect? Well, you're stopping your creativity and yourself with your self-limiting attitude. Don't analyze until you're paralyzed. Be courageous and creative, not perfect.

On the Couch

"The greatest mistake you can make is to be
continually fearing you will make one."
—ELBERT HUBBARD

Janet was a perfectionist who was so hard on herself that no matter what she wrote, she put herself down and berated herself unmercifully. She was an overachiever who was constantly taking on new challenges in her writing, but they never were good enough to satisfy her.

In her personal life she had a number of failed relationships that followed a similar pattern. Eventually, she drove men away with her perfectionist behavior and critical attitude towards them. Her perfectionism was not only related to her writing, but also to her relationships with others.

She had been in analysis for five years when she attended one of my writing workshops. In those sessions she was depressed, weepy, and cried every time she read her stories, which were reminiscences from her childhood. She came to see me a couple of weeks after that and said she wanted to work on some issues about her childhood that had arisen in the workshop through her writings. She was in a state of confusion and felt completely desolate when I first saw her for therapy.

"I'm blown away at the childhood memories that came up for me during the class. I realized in your workshop that my need to be perfect started as a kid. It was also very hard for me to do your method writing. I couldn't let go of trying to be in control of my writing. I felt so depressed that I couldn't even feel free when doing a writing exercise where there weren't any rules or expectations."

Janet went on to explain that she never had any rest from her perfectionist self. "From the moment I start to write to the time I go to bed, I have to listen to a voice that criticizes me and my writing."

"What does the voice tell you? I asked. "Write a list of what it's saying right now."

She hesitated and finally began to write in her notebook:

"You can't write."
"Your writing is mediocre."
"You're ridiculous."
"You'll never be a good writer."

"No wonder you don't enjoy writing. The voice defeats you before you even begin," I said.

"Yes, the voice criticizes me on everything I write. It doesn't matter whether or not I'm writing my screenplay or writing ads for the agency, where I'm a copywriter."

"That must be exhausting."

"It is. When my creative director likes my copy, I don't believe him. I still think it isn't good enough, or that perhaps I could have done better. When I'm working on my screenplay even the subject doesn't seem important, because I just can't write."

"Always striving for the impossible and never reaching it with your writing must make you depressed and disappointed."

"It doesn't. Most of all it saps my creative energy when I get stuck and stop myself."

"You've got to learn that there's no such thing as 'perfect.' We're going to work on how you can be comfortable with not being perfect. Otherwise, you'll stop yourself and never succeed in reaching your writing goals."

Together, we began the search for the cause of her perfectionism in all aspects of Janet's life.

Off the Couch

"Judge each day not by the harvest you reap but by the seeds you plant."
—ROBERT LOUIS STEVENSON

When Janet came in for her session each week, we delved into the search for reasons for her perfectionism. She still wasn't able to let up on herself and to just experience the writing process. As much as she tried to release herself from the bondage of her perfectionism, she was as critical as always.

"Just knowing the reason you behave a certain way doesn't necessarily help you change your behavior," I told her.

"You're right. I thought I'd stop being so self-critical after I identified my mother as the person who was the cause of my needing to be perfect as a kid."

I explained that many writers want to figure out why they have problems writing, but that doesn't take care of the cure. The why is just the beginning of change; it's the action you take as a result of your new understanding that causes new behaviors. "It takes courage to be wrong and to take risks in your writing. I believe your childhood fear of making a mistake is at the root of your problem. This week I don't want you to edit your writing. Just get it down as quickly as you can without trying to be perfect."

"That's so difficult for me. I don't know if I can change."

"Yes, you can. Just let go of your need to be perfect. It's a killer and limits you as a writer as well as stunts your creativity," I said.

"That's why I'm here, because I haven't been able to let it go even though I've tried."

As we continued our work, I discovered that Janet constantly wanted her parents' approval. She got it when she accomplished tasks and did a "job well done," as her father always said.

I encouraged Janet to let go of all the writing rules and just ignore the critical voice and find delight with her creativity.

"When you write, be a playful little kid who has fun with the words and plays with the writing. In fact, I want you to write as badly as you can."

"What do you mean?" she asked quizzically.

"Loosen up, and lose your perfectionism. Try to be second best. It is impossible to always be perfect. You're only human, so be humane to yourself and let it go."

"What can I do about my writing?"

"As I said, just write as bad as you can. Don't worry about mistakes, spelling, grammar, or content. I don't want you to put any pressure on yourself for fear of making a mistake. Mistakes are good."

She looked at me and asked, "How bad is writing bad?"

"You're such a perfectionist that you have to be the best bad writer you can be."

She laughed.

At first it was very difficult for Janet to write as bad as she could. But she didn't give up and kept trying I found that if I had her write during our session as fast as she could without stopping, and egging her on, she didn't have time to be judgmental about her writing. I watched her as she wrote and noted that it was really a painful process for her to let go. As I studied her body language when she was writing as bad as she could, it was evident that she was terrified, uncomfortable, and scared because she wasn't being perfect. She struggled with being free and playful while writing.

We did several writing exercises, and each time she became less and less rigid and restrictive and more playful. Soon she looked forward to these writing sessions. I saw that she was relaxed as she continued writing as fast as she could. I recognized a new freedom within her because of the writing exercises we had done.

As she started to let go more and more of her need for perfectionism, I told her, "Have the courage to make mistakes. Be real and don't be right, just write it."

During the following weeks, Janet's transformation was dramatic. She relaxed and loosened up in both her personal and professional life. She was happier and enjoyed working on her screenplay so much that she finished it in less than a month because she wasn't trying to be perfect. She felt greatly relieved and was thrilled that she didn't have to beat herself up anymore or be critical of other people if they weren't perfect. The good news is her screenplay found a home with a small production company.

Shrink Rap

Writing bad is good.
Being perfect is bad.
Stop trying to write it perfect,
And you won't end up feeling sad.

Creativity Chronicle

"Better to do something imperfectly than to do nothing flawlessly."
—ROBERT H. SCHULLER

Circumvent your perfectionism and that voice that says you aren't good enough by writing as bad as you possibly can. Use Ballon Method Writing™ to write about your need for control, your belief that you are never good enough, and your tendency to critically judge yourself all the time. Remember, write as bad as you can and trust your intuition. Next, write a page or two of your short story, screenplay, novel, play, or nonfiction book. Just get it down, without editing, rewriting, or being a perfectionist.

SHRINK WRAP-UP: UNTIL NEXT TIME

- Remember that there's no such thing as being a perfect writer.
- Let go of your perfectionism in your writing and just write it any way you can.
- Don't try to be a perfect writer. Be a productive writer.

SESSION 14

I'm Not Good Enough

"Self-trust is the first secret of success."
—RALPH WALDO EMERSON

You are *not* your writing. If you want to be a successful writer, you need to separate yourself from your writing when it's criticized or rejected. Otherwise, your self-esteem will always be based on the reactions your writing gets from publishers, teachers, editors, producers, directors, agents, and peers.

When other people love your writing, does your self-esteem increase? Conversely, if somebody you don't even know rejects your writing, do you feel low self-esteem? You can't let the vicissitudes of other people's opinions determine how you feel about yourself and your writing. You need to know who you are apart from your writing; otherwise, your creativity and your confidence will always be dependent on other people.

This is not a good way of being because rejection is just another part of the writing process. You can't take it personally—that is, if you feel you've done the best writing you can do and you've gotten feedback from other writers you respect, before you send it out you'll then believe in what you've written even if it gets rejected.

I tell the writers I coach that rejection means only one thing: that they're not buying what you're selling. It's as simple as that. If you're selling apples and they want pears, it doesn't make your apple any less of an apple; it's just that they wanted pears. Don't take the rejection personally, but be professional enough to continue sending out your apple.

If you want to be published or produced, you need to look at writing as a business. You must be courageous enough to keep sending out your manuscript or your script instead of going into a deep funk or feeling sorry for yourself. As a writer, you need to have balance in your life and get fulfillment apart from your writing. Self-care isn't being selfish; rather, it means developing a healthier ego so you don't get down on yourself when your writing is rejected. Otherwise, you'll stop the first time you get a rejection letter or no letter at all.

To be a writer is to be rejected. I'm not kidding. Those writers who stop writing the first time they're rejected can't call themselves writers because rejection is part and parcel of the writing game. It isn't what happens to you if you're rejected, it's what you do or don't do *when* you're rejected. Turn rejection into an opportunity to learn something about your writing. If along with the rejection you've also been given good notes or comments, pay attention. Take what you need and disregard the rest, or disregard everything if you don't agree. The important thing is to be professional enough to not take rejection personally, just professionally.

In therapy I help my clients learn to appreciate all the good things about themselves rather than tuning into the constant mental chatter about how awful, terrible, and horrible they are. You can be the most talented creative writer in the world, but if you don't have confidence in or esteem for yourself, you may as well give up now. Writing is not only about dealing with rejection it's also about writing, rewriting, and more rewriting.

Don't be fragile or faint of heart in the face of rejection. Develop a thick skin, and keep on keeping on. Develop coping skills in advance for your writing and for selling it. See a therapist to learn to appreciate yourself from the inside out if you're having problems coping with rejection if it's affecting your overall well-being. Expect rejection and disappointments with the knowledge that you'll recover from them. Be just as prepared for rejection as you're prepared for an earthquake in California or a hurricane in Florida. This planning takes courage and commitment in order for you to increase your self-worth as a writer. Build up your mental attitude by preparing for all types of disappointments and rejections in advance until you get to "yes."

On the Couch

No one can disgrace us but ourselves."
—J. G. HOLLAND

Betsy, a playwright, came to see me because she had been having anxiety attacks. Recently, she had sent out her latest full-length play to regional theaters, and now she was waiting for responses.

"I've always had what I call 'submission anxiety,'" Betsy said during our first session. "But now I have anxiety all the time."

"What does 'submission anxiety' mean to you?" I asked.

"Well, after I send out my play, I just can't live with waiting to be rejected. When I first started writing plays, I guess I had what you call beginner's luck. The second theater I sent my one-act to accepted it and even put it on in an evening of one-act plays. So with my full-length play I was hopeful when I first started to send it out. But after getting rejected so many times, I feel depressed, and I'm just marking time waiting for another rejection. I become anxiety-ridden, and now I don't even send my play out to theaters that are waiting for it."

"Why are you so certain you'll be rejected?"

"Because lately I have been. It has just destroyed my self-confidence so much that I hate the whole process. The time it takes between submitting my writing and waiting for an answer is unbearable. I just can't live with the ambiguity anymore. I can't handle it."

Betsy's negative and fearful attitude toward rejection wasn't only based on her writing, it was the fallout of her own feelings of low self-esteem. Rather than concentrating on her feelings about getting rejected, when sending her material out, I focused on helping her build up her self-esteem in general.

Off the Couch

"A man who finds no satisfaction in himself, seeks for it in vain elsewhere."
—FRANÇOIS LA ROUCHEFOUCAULD

As we worked together on the insecure aspect of her personality, I gave Betsy some writing assignments dealing with her feelings of low self-esteem. She wrote about the first time she recalled feeling insecure and found it had nothing to do with her writing. Here is what Betsy wrote:

"My friend Suzie and I are playing at her house. We play with all of her dolls and it is so much fun to pretend the different dolls are our girlfriends. They are going to have a party. Suzie is my best friend and we sing songs together as she plays the piano. Her mother is so nice to us and always makes us lunch. I love the bologna sandwiches she makes and the cokes we're allowed to drink at her house. In my house we're not allowed to drink anything with our meals. Only water after we finish. At Suzie's house we have fun. We're in the middle of playing with her doll collection when the doorbell rings. I wonder who it is and suddenly Nancy, another friend of Suzie's, enters the room. She ignores me and doesn't even say hello. I'm upset because I wanted Suzie all to myself and she didn't tell me Nancy was coming over. I get quiet as the two of them laugh and play and I feel so small as they continue to ignore me. I can't believe Suzie would rather be with that loud, mean Nancy, than with me. But after a while it's clear she doesn't even know I'm there. I feel angry and upset, but try not to show it. Finally Nancy turns to me and says, "What's the matter with you?"

I know I shouldn't say anything, but my lips begin to quiver and I say, "I thought I was the only one playing with Suzie today." It is a stupid thing to say, but I feel so alone that I just blurt it out without thinking.

Nancy laughs. "Don't you know that two's company and three's a crowd? Why don't you leave?" I am so shocked that I can't move.

I wait for Suzie, my best friend, to take my part and ask Nancy to leave, but she just laughs along with Nancy and they both stare at me as I gather my things while fighting the tears. Suzie still doesn't ask me to stay. I don't say anything or do anything, but just quietly get up to go. Nancy immediately takes the doll I had been playing with and starts to play with it. Suzie lets her. My best friend watches without a word, a goodbye or anything, while I leave the room to go home.

From that day on, my self-esteem was shattered and I've never been able to trust that anyone will really be my friend no matter what."

As Betsy read what she had written, she was amazed that she had written about that childhood incident as a time of feeling bad about herself. We talked about the fact that she'd done nothing wrong. Her friend and Nancy were the ones who were mean. Betsy's bad feelings that weren't about anything she'd done.

I told her, "Betsy, I know you felt rejected about what happened, but you didn't cause Nancy to be mean nor was it your fault that your best friend didn't defend you."

She said, "Even though I know it's true, I don't understand why I wrote about that particular incident, when I haven't thought about it in years. Besides, I know how mean kids can be to one another."

"Right now you're being logical and analytical, but I believe you're still affected by this childhood incident of being rejected and it still influences your lack of trusting others. We need to work on the fact that after being rejected with your writing you still need to believe and trust yourself. This isn't the same rejection you experienced when you were a kid, even though it might feel like it."

As we continued to work on Betsy's feelings of self-esteem, she eventually realized how unrealistic it was to feel personally rejected when her writing was rejected. She was being hypersensitive and had let childhood rejection affect her feelings about herself and her confidence. Through our work together, she soon discovered that by increasing her self-esteem she was also able to increase her creative output.

As Betsy started to have more confidence, she gained the ability to separate herself from her writing. Eventually, she even stopped experiencing "submission anxiety." The solution to her anxiety was the discovery that the problem was within her, and dealing with that issue was the solution to her "submission anxiety." If we had only concentrated on discussing her feelings regarding rejection, we never would have succeeded in helping her overcome her feelings of low self-esteem and Betsy would still be suffering from inner anxiety about her writing.

Betsy now has no problem being a professional writer who knows that rejection is just a part of the writing process. She knows that she is separate from her writing. She's now a person with confidence and esteem, and her submission anxiety was just a manifestation of her insecurity and lack of faith in herself. Happily, her play was eventually accepted and produced in a small regional theater—something that would never have happened unless she had overcome her submission anxiety.

She now recognizes her talent and the ability that is inherent within her. Betsy is also more successful in her relationships because she now values who she is and her creative spirit.

Shrink Rap

When your writing gets rejected just remember not to feel dejected.
Remember, they're buying pears, and your selling apples.

Creativity Chronicle

The kind of life is most happy which affords
us most opportunities of gaining our own esteem."
—SAMUEL JOHNSON

Using the Ballon Method Writing,™ create a 'Creativity Brag Page." Write down everything you can think of about yourself that you're either proud of or that you do well. It doesn't have to do with writing. It can be something such as the following:

"I'm a good friend."
"I bake a mean chocolate cake."
"I'm an avid reader."
"I appreciate jazz."
"I'm a terrific tennis player."

Write down at least ten or more of your positive traits, and be sure to keep adding to the list, which is your creativity brag page. Read your list over daily, especially when you need a booster shot of self-esteem or when your writing gets rejected.

SHRINK WRAP-UP: UNTIL NEXT TIME

- Trust your gut feeling when you start writing, and believe in yourself.
- Keep adding good things about yourself to your Creativity Brag Page.
- You are good enough just the way you are; don't quit submitting your writing even when it gets rejected.

SESSION 15

The Dog Ate My First Draft

"He who never made a mistake never made a discovery."
—SAMUEL SMILES

Excuses are the same as self-fulfilling prophecies. If you continue to make excuses for not writing, you will end up failing in your writing. Why? That's because you'll allow excuses to keep you from doing what you need to do—WRITE! The negative power of making excuses isn't limited to writing and increasing creativity. Excuse making can permeate every area of your life. If you allow yourself off the hook because of excuses, you'll never achieve your dreams or reach your goals.

Do your excuses stop you in other areas of your life as well? Do you make excuses before you even *try* to write? Are excuses ruining your life, not only in writing but also in other important parts of your life?

When did you start to make excuses instead of doing what you needed to do? Did your excuses start in childhood? Are you lazy, or are you scared? Are you hiding behind your excuses to be safe? Do you make excuses to stay in your "comfort zone?" Are you making excuses because you're afraid of the unknown? Do you always sabotage yourself with your excuses?

In order to overcome them, it's important for you to investigate the reasons you make excuses for yourself. You can't change what you aren't aware of. Therefore, you need to identify when and why you began to offer excuses for not writing, rather than taking the action in the first place.

On the Couch

Character is that which can do without success.
—RALPH WALDO EMERSON

Quite a few of my writing clients have become successful. Others drift back into their old habits and never overcome their problems. One of the major differences I've noticed between the two groups is making excuses. Those who succeed as writers, write, and those who don't succeed don't write. They make excuses.

Shannon was a student in my writing workshop. She never did the homework, which was always some specific writing assignment to be completed the following week. Each week I'd hear excuses about why she hadn't been able to do the assignments; when I spoke to her about it, she made an appointment to see me. She was angry because she didn't think I understood her situation, even though she hadn't completed half of her writing assignments. I asked her if she was willing to work or whether she wanted to continue to make excuses for not turning in her writing assignments. I had given her several extensions, but at this point I felt she was taking advantage and told her so.

"I'm trying to do my best, but I have a husband and a child to deal with as well as school and it's just so hard. I wish you and the other teachers would understand. I'm so tired that I can't seem to come up with any creative ideas about which to write."

"That's up to you, Shannon, but the price you're paying for allowing yourself to always make excuses for not writing, is probably higher than making an effort to do the writing."

"Well, you don't seem to realize that I'm doing my best, but I only have so much time."

It seemed that talking to Shannon was like talking to the wall. Making excuses was such a large part of her life that she truly believed her own stories.

I pointed that out to her. "If you put some of your energy into doing your assignments, rather than into the excuses for not doing them, you'll end up with feelings of well-being, pride, and competence. Shannon, don't continue to put yourself in the position of always having to explain why you don't do your assignments."

She was so busy with her excuses and obviously didn't want to change. The following excuses are just a sample of what I heard throughout the course:

"I had to work late."
"My kid was sick."
"I was too tired."
"I had other commitments."

Off the Couch

"A man's own character is the arbiter of his fortune."
—SYRUS

At the next session with Shannon, I said, "Maybe these were valid reasons and maybe not, but after hearing them every time you didn't turn in an assignment they sound more like excuses than reasons."

She began to protest, but I continued. "Do you know why? Because there are others in the class who have children and they do the writing. And mostly everyone comes to class directly from work and they're just as tired as you. But the other students manage to get their writing assignments done."

"Well, I don't know what to say, but I wish you'd understand I can't do it all."

I decided not to discuss the matter with Shannon but to make a new rule that I put into place immediately for the students who were taking the class for credit. I would allow only one assignment to be turned in late. No excuses would be accepted, and if homework wasn't turned in, it would affect their grade. At first I heard complaint after complaint from Shannon. But it didn't take long before all that energy that in the past had been expended on making excuses began to be redirected toward a positive change of behavior. Because getting a good grade was important to her, Shannon started turning her assignments in on time and stopped complaining. By the end of the class, it was obvious she felt good about herself as she turned in the work. She made an appointment to see me and to my surprise, thanked me for instituting that new rule in the workshop.

"I know now that you were right. I really do feel better about myself and want to thank you for calling me on my excuses. You helped me learn to be accountable and in fact I even have more time than I ever had when I didn't do the work."

By forcing Shannon to finally suffer the consequences of making excuses by making a strict rule regarding the writing assignments, I helped her become a better writer. At the same time, she also developed more energy for the writing itself and for her creativity. She felt good about herself for doing the work and proud of her writing.

Shrink Rap

No excuses. No excuses. No excuses. No excuses.
No excuses. No excuses. No excuses. No excuses.

Creativity Chronicle

"The only courage that matters is the kind that
gets you from one moment to the next."
—MIGNON MCLAUGHLIN

Make a list of all the excuses you have for not writing. Write them down as fast as you can. Read them over. Are they actual valid reasons or are they lame excuses? Circle the ones that are excuses and write about how you can get rid of your excuses and take an action.

SHRINK WRAP-UP: UNTIL NEXT TIME

- Put the energy it takes to make excuses into your writing.
- Learn to be accountable for getting your writing projects completed on time.
- Remember, writers write; people who make excuses don't.

SESSION 16

Success Will Ruin Me

"Keep your fears to yourself but share your courage with others."
—ROBERT LOUISE STEVENSON

S uccess is a state of mind. It is failure turned around. It's the mystique of success and the allure of success that most writers want, but few of us believe we can reach. There are many reasons we don't achieve the success we personally want, reasons of which we're unaware.

Fear of success is often programmed in childhood by parents who inadvertently give their children the message never to exceed them. Because of these childhood messages, many of you sabotage your own success, unaware that you're doing it. You might believe you just aren't as lucky as others, when in reality you're the one stopping yourself from being successful.

Sounds crazy, doesn't it? But it's true. You want success and yet you stop yourself from achieving it. Does the saying "You are your own worst enemy" hit a nerve? Here are some of the unconscious negative messages that you probably bombard yourself with regarding success:

"I get so scared when things start to go well."
"My success happened by accident."
"Nobody likes people who win."
"I don't want them to hate me if I become successful."
"If they only knew I can't do it again."

These inner negative voices keep you from achieving success without your ever being aware of them. You see it takes courage to be successful. In fact, it takes courage to be successful in any aspect of your life. But it really takes courage to send out your writing again and again after it's been rejected. The difference between successful and unsuccessful writers is courage. Do you have the courage to do something that you're scared to do? Do you have the courage to take a risk and send out your writing? Do you have the courage to even fail and try and try over and over and over again?

Don't stop yourself because you fear you won't be successful. To proceed is to succeed. To stop is to *not*. It's your choice. Go for it.

On the Couch

"Half the things that people do not succeed in are through fear of making the attempt."
—JAMES NORTHCOTE

Nancy, a freelance comedy writer, became a client when she couldn't access her comic self and ideas in her new job as a sitcom staff writer. She was under a lot of pressure to prove herself, as there were more experienced writers on the show. In the beginning she was holding her own.

"I was really getting comfortable with the other writers," Nancy said. "They seemed to like my jokes and a few told me they were impressed with my humor."

"So what happened to change all that? Why are you now blocked?"

"Everything changed when my new boss, Donna, an older writer, came on board. I don't know what happened, but when Donna was in the room, I froze up and couldn't be funny.

"Why do you think you became so scared?" I asked.

"I don't know why, but I just always lose my confidence when she's around. Last week I became so anxious that I couldn't get ready for work without throwing up."

We discussed the fact that she was not singled out for criticism and that her boss also criticized the other writers.

"In the room where all of us writers get together every day to discuss each week's episode, I'm quiet."

"Why is that happening now, when earlier you told me you were complimented on your humor?"

"I can't be funny on demand, when Donna is waiting for me to say something clever. I just close off and become a mute. No matter how I rehearse ideas and new jokes, when I get into the studio I clam up. I don't know why when things are good I get scared."

"Perhaps it's easier for you not to succeed. It sounds like when you start to be successful you become extremely anxious."

She was desperate. "It's true that I get nervous, but if I don't start performing I'm going to get fired and I really need this job."

Off the Couch

"It is hard to fail, but it is worse never to have tried to succeed."
—THEODORE ROOSEVELT

During the next session I asked her, "Why do you seem to be sabotaging yourself just as you're heading toward writing success?"

She was surprised with the question. "I don't know if I am."

"Do you recall ever feeling the same way in your childhood that you now feel on the sitcom?

She thought for a few minutes and said, "In my family, my mother would always make me feel guilty, when I came home from a date and had a great time. She'd say, 'I'm glad someone in this house can have fun.'"

"How did that make you feel?"

"I felt guilty because my mother never seemed happy. When I went to college and made the dean's list the first semester, I rushed home to tell her and she said something like 'Well, at least you're able to go to college, which is something more than I could do. I wasn't as privileged as you.'"

As we talked she told me how guilty she was made to feel by her mother.

"Maybe it was easier not to succeed than it was to make your mother upset."

She looked at me surprised. "Wow! I know that I felt depressed when Mother was sad. In fact, I always felt guilty, too."

"Do you think it's possible you unconsciously decided not to succeed so your mother wouldn't be jealous?"

"That seems ridiculous. After all, I haven't stopped trying."

"That's true, but it seems as if you're terrified now to succeed. Do you think Donna has anything to do with it? Does she remind you of your mother?"

Nancy thought about what I'd said for quite a while. "Maybe she does. I know that my mother was easier to get along with when she wasn't mad at me because of my successes."

"And even though you feel pressured by Donna, your need not to succeed that you learned from your mother is what stops you."

Nancy nodded. "Yes, I felt much better with the other writers before Donna came on board, and she's older like my mother."

In time Nancy was able to work through her guilt and fear of success by doing Ballon Method Writing™ exercises and changing her feelings of fear to feelings of joy from her creativity. As she started to embrace her success on the page through writing, she was soon able to embrace her success on the sitcom. Her fear of success decreased as her confidence in herself increased. Luckily, she discovered her inner fear and was able to change. She was asked to return the following year, not only as a writer but also as a story editor.

Shrink Rap

You're a winner, a winner, a winner, a winner.
You can proceed, succeed, achieve, succeed.

Creativity Chronicle

Courage is resistance to fear, mastery of fear, not absence of fear."
—MARK TWAIN

Picture yourself as if you have already achieved your writing goals. Visualize your success in vivid detail with all of your senses. Imagine how you feel being a successful writer. Now write for twenty minutes in great detail about your experience of being a successful writer.

SHRINK WRAP-UP: UNTIL NEXT TIME

- Learn to embrace and welcome success.
- Recognize and let go of your own resistance that stops you from becoming a successful writer.
- Remember not to hold yourself back when you've almost reached the finish line.

SESSION 17

The IMAWRITAMAYBENOT Monologues

"You are searching for the magic key that will unlock the door to the source of power; and yet you have the key in your own hands, and you may use it the moment you learn to control your thoughts.."
—NAPOLEON HILL

D
o you have reruns of negative tapes playing in your head day and night? Do they drown out any positive hopes, dreams, or aspirations of being a writer? If the answer is yes, these are the negative monologues and the destructive dialogues that you have unconsciously integrated as part of your inner landscape. They are like weeds that constantly destroy your beautiful ideas and creative concepts, before they can ever get safely planted on the page and rooted in your writing.

Do you have any idea where these negative mantras came from? How did they become so powerful and loud? Since you can't change anything without first being aware of it, let's look at their origin and how they first developed.

As children, many of you were given negative injunctions by parents, teachers, and caregivers:

"You can't do that."
"Don't touch this."

"No."

"Be quiet."

Many of these messages were necessary to protect you when you were still too young to look after yourself. They were often the only way your parents knew to keep you from getting hurt or in trouble. They were also necessary things for you to learn so that you could be socialized in order to become a productive member of society. Unfortunately, most of them are negative.

Almost by definition, child rearing instills negative messages from parents. And over the years, you learn to incorporate these negative monologues into your psyche. Your parents most likely weren't intentionally being cruel, mean, or critical; they were just doing what parents do—helping you to develop acceptable behavior, follow the rules, and be integrated into society. Unfortunately, the constant negative teaching eventually dampens your spirit and transforms you from a free, wild child into a child dominated by "shoulds," have to's," "need to's," "can'ts," "don'ts," and so on.

As you grew older, the messages often got worse and more destructive, especially once you became a teenager. Suddenly, in order to guide you to act appropriately, the messages became more about ridicule and criticism. Even if you argued or fought back, unconsciously you tended to integrate these critical messages into your personality. They became a part of your negative monologues and destructive dialogues. Today, those negative tapes are still playing, and they prevent you from succeeding, give you low self-esteem, and often make you feel hopeless.

On the Couch

"I write entirely to find out what I'm thinking...
"What I want, and what I fear."
—JOAN DIDION

I started my weekly writer's support group for writers who wanted to deal with their emotions and their frame of mind regarding their writing. Writers need all the support they can get, and this group provided them with emotional and psychological support in order to better deal with personal and professional writing issues.

Each week, we discussed barriers to writing that are often focused on issues such as overcoming procrastination, increasing creativity and productivity, and dealing with fear of rejection/failure/success.

However, the negative monologues and destructive dialogues that writers in my weekly writer's support group have identified as problem areas are the most pervasive type of obstacle to creative flow. Recently, I had each member write down some of the negative monologues they had to struggle against. Here are some of the most common:

> "Don't be stupid."
> "Why can't you get anything right?"
> "You're so clumsy."
> "Why do you always do such dumb things?"

As we went around the room, the individual lists were endless and had a lot of similarities. However, since the most pervasive blocks to creativity are due to the internal dialogues within each writer, we dealt with negative monologues and destructive dialogues that prevented each from being the best writer he or she could be, because of fears.

It's almost impossible to increase creativity and prime the creative pump, when the debris of destructive dialogues and negative monologues chokes off creative ideas. I had everyone in the group write a list of negative self-talk they heard loud and clear when they started to write. See if you can relate to any of these negative monologues:

> "I'm not sensitive."
> "I can't write fiction."
> "I have no creativity."
> "My ideas are stupid."
> "My writing sucks."

I had each writer try to identify the person who said these negative statements to them long ago. It was amazing how different versions of similar negative themes there were inside of each writer.

Off the Couch

"No one can make you feel inferior without your consent."
—ELEANOR ROOSEVELT

The following week, the writers returned with their list of negative statements and the identity of the person who criticized them. One client realized that his father always made snide remarks in an off-handed manner, but they still were powerful and wielded a poisonous sting. He shared some of the most hurtful ones:

"You can't be a writer."
"You never were clever."
"Writing isn't real work."

Another member identified her negative monologues as coming from her critical grandmother. She had written down some of the negative messages she had received when she announced she was going to be a writer.

"Stop wasting your time and be responsible."
"Ibsen was a real writer."
"Get a good paying job."
"Stop dreaming your life away."

After she identified these messages as coming from her grandmother, I told her to then refute what was said to her. She wrote the following monologue:

"I am a creative writer. I may not be Ibsen, but I'm a good writer. Writing is a wonderful profession, and I'm glad I chose it. As a writer I work hard and am responsible and accountable. I love writing more than anything else and I have no intention of ever stopping. And by the way, I think everything you said to me that was mean and stupid is because you were jealous of me. So there!"

These refutations helped her overcome the constant critical voices that she had integrated as her own voice.

When you identify the negative monologues and identify the messenger by becoming aware of who said them, you start the healing process by changing these negative monologues from the past that stopped you, into positive monologues that encourage you. The good news is that by changing your monologues from negative to positive, you can change yourself from being negative to being positive about your writing as well as your life.

Shrink Rap

Destructive dialogue: *You're not a writer.*
Positive Dialogue: *Yes I am.*
Negative Monologue: *You aren't a creative person.*
Positive Monologue: *Shut up! Be quiet! Go away! I'm not listening.*

Creativity Chronicle

*"Our minds can shape the way a thing will be
because we act according to our expectations."*
—FREDERICO FELLINI

Stop your negative chatter by writing in your Creativity Chronicle every time you hear a negative monologue whispering to you. Stop it in its tracks before the whisper becomes a shout. Keep notes by jotting down each and every destructive dialogue or negative monologue you hear throughout the day.

Then try to identify the voice(s) screaming these deadly messages at you. Is it your fifth-grade teacher, your mother, your father, a friend, sister, brother? Afterwards, rewrite these negative monologues to positive ones and let the person(s) know they've lost their power to discourage you and make you feel bad about yourself and your writing ability. For example, you can change a negative message by refuting it, like this:

"You're lazy."

"No, that's not true. I'm not a lazy person. I work hard."

Elaborate your refutations even more when you write a response to the criticisms you've heard in the past. Empower yourself as you cross out all the negative monologues. Then, for 21 days read the positive messages before you go to bed and as soon as you awaken. This is the time it takes to change old thoughts and accept new ones. This will allow you to free yourself from chains of the past that constantly tie you up and hold your creative spirit hostage. Open up your world and your vocabulary about yourself and change the words, so you can go from feeling negative to feeling like a positive writer and a person.

SHRINK WRAP-UP: UNTIL NEXT TIME

- Keep a list of all the negative monologues and destructive dialogues you tell yourself throughout the day and night. Then use whiteout to erase all the negative messages.
- Tell yourself every day that you're a writer and a darn good one.
- Write down the top ten reasons you know to call yourself a good writer.

SESSION 18

Why Did I Ever Think I could Write a Script/Novel/Poem/Play/Haiku?

"Nothing succeeds like a failure."
—OLIVER HERFORD

Your fears can keep you stuck in a rut and prevent you from reaching your writing goals. On the one hand, you want to be published or produced; on the other, you let your fears stop you. When you think about what will happen to your writing, you probably imagine the worst-case scenario, and your creativity gets dried up as your fears flood your imagination. Staying stuck in your fears keeps you stuck in your writing as well as in your life. Think about your reasons for staying stuck. Are you waiting for someone to stand over your shoulder and make you finish? Don't wait for anyone to rescue you because they won't. If you're waiting for an editor or a literary agent to call you and say, "I'm waiting for you to finish your novel, please get it to me as quickly as you can," it's time to realize that that's a fantasy. It won't happen.

Nobody has a larger stake in your writing than you do. Nobody can stop your fear of failure except you. Nobody can enhance your creativity but you. And all it takes is taking hold of your fear of failure and putting it on the shelf.

Are you willing to take a risk in your writing and in your creativity? It's all up to you. How? By doing what you fear to do. That's right—you need to complete your writing and send it out in spite of your fears. Your own resistance to your fears will grow as you focus on them. So just ignore them. Have the courage to stop living in fear.

Don't allow negative emotions to control your life. Jump over your fears with faith in yourself and a belief in your writing.

There's no such thing as failure. There is such a thing as stopping too soon, before you have time to let yourself succeed. Replace your fears with faith. Take stock of your fears, recognize them, and then put them away in a bag in the back of your closet.

Fear is a perception that you have the freedom to change. Change your fear to excitement, and let your fearful energy turn into creative energy. Embrace your fears rather than fighting them. Make friends with your fears; don't try to disown them, or they will come back to haunt you. When fears arise before or during your writing, say to yourself, "Oh, you're doing it again. Just be quiet and let me write." And just *write*, in spite of your fears.

Whenever you begin to worry about failing, read this poem. Hopefully it will inspire you.

Don't Be Afraid to Fail
You've failed many times, although you may not remember.
You fell down the first time you tried to walk.
You almost drowned the first time you tried to swim, didn't you?
Did you hit the ball the first time you swung a bat?
Heavy hitters, the ones who hit the most home runs, also strike out a lot.
R.H. Macy failed seven times before his store in New York caught on.
English novelist John Creasey got 753 rejection slips before he published 564 books.
Babe Ruth struck out 1,330 times, but he also hit 714 home runs.
                                                                —Unknown

On the Couch

"Action is the last resource of those who know not how to dream."
—OSCAR WILDE

Martin, a seasoned journalist, came to see me after he had been blocked for over a year from writing his novel. "I have a big fear quotient—fear of self, fear of rejection, fear of failure, fear of success. I'm always fighting my internal fears. I suppose a lot of them are mostly imagined, but I can't seem to change."

He was in his early forties and really wanted to become a working novelist. "I have three children and a mortgage to make every month, and I am afraid all the time. When I start to work on my novel I think, 'Why bother, I'll be rejected anyway.' Or I tell myself that I'm just wasting my time, when I should be earning money for my family."

"You certainly have a lot of pressure," I said. "It sounds as if your fears are interfering with your writing."

"And I have every reason to have these fears. I hate my job, and have no idea how long I can stand it since the paper has a new editor. She and I just don't hit it off."

As Martin recited all of his fears, I realized it was no wonder that he couldn't write. He was afraid he'd be fired; he worried about money and his marriage, which was under more strain as he was under more tension. "I've got to somehow stop worrying about my novel. I haven't worked on it for months."

I gave him writing assignments each week. At first I had him write some childhood scenes about how he enjoyed being free and spontaneous. When he read the stories out loud to me in our sessions, he always ended up feeling happy. "It's been so long since I felt free and creative that I really enjoyed getting back to those times in childhood. It seems so long ago."

Even though he seemed more relaxed, the "fearful voices" still haunted him night and day. He began to get angry with them and to realize what a drain it was to listen to them, not only on his energy but also on his self-esteem and confidence.

Off the Couch

"Courage faces fear and thereby masters it."
—MARTIN LUTHER KING, JR.

"I want you to make a note of every time the fearful voices block you in your creative writing and to write down what they are shouting at you during the day and night," I said.

When Martin returned, he had written two pages of fears that he had. Although some were based in reality, many of them were irrational. Here are some of Martin's fears:

"I'm afraid nobody will buy my work."
"I don't think I can complete my writing."
"What if my writing isn't good?"
"No publisher will like what I write."

I told Martin that without a guarantee, no writers are sure that what they write will ever be published or produced. "All of your fears could come true, but how can you write in spite of them?"

"I don't know, but I really do want to write," he said.

"Well, until you can break through your fears and become passionate about your writing, you'll continue to let them stop you."

"What can I do?" he asked.

I then had him read over his fears and try to change them into excitement or opportunities and to challenge them in his writing.

The next week he came back with the same list of fears but now he challenged them.

"I'm afraid nobody will buy my work."

He wrote challenges as follows.

"It doesn't matter if I'm not guaranteed that someone will buy my writing because I believe in what I'm writing so I'm not going to stop."

"I don't think I can complete my writing."

"I have the power to finish my writing and I plan on writing until I complete my novel."

"What if my writing isn't good?"

"My writing is good because I write from my passion and I've studied the craft. I also have enough faith in myself and my writing ability to know what is good writing."

"No publisher will like what I write."

"I'm hopeful and believe that when I finish my novel I'll get a publisher who will want to buy it."

Through not accepting his fears, but challenging them, Martin's fearful voice gradually receded and became less intense and he became less rigid and uptight about his writing.

As he reconnected to his courageous self, by challenging his fears, he transformed from a frightened adult into a courageous one. I also started to notice that he exuded an air of confidence that I had not seen before, in the early days of his therapy. One day he said, "You know, writing down my fears and seeing how irrational most of them were was great for me, because I had forgotten how brave I used to be. Listing my fears and realizing how I had become fear-based has helped me overcome them. I've even noticed that this hasn't been limited to just my fears in my writing, but has spilled over into my personal life as well. People seem to want to be engaged with me now, more than they did when I was full of fears."

Instead of focusing on Martin's novel or using our therapy time to simply help him write it, I concentrated on Martin's fears and by refuting them he was able to get in touch with his creative self rather than his fearful self. This turned out to be the best strategy. When he left therapy, he was halfway finished with his novel, had quit his job, and had begun a new one that he loved. He's also a more confident person—not only with his writing, but in his life as well.

Shrink rap

Fear stands for:

Frustration
Envy
Anxiety
Resentment

Creativity Chronicle

"Act as if it were impossible to fail."
—DOROTHEA BRANDE

Write down a list of all your fears, especially those that stop you from unleashing your creativity through your writing. Now visualize yourself as taking a risk in your writing in spite of your fears. Write about being successful in your writing because of your courage to write, and overcome your fears.

SHRINK WRAP-UP: UNTIL NEXT TIME

- Face your fears and write in spite of them.
- The more you do the things you're afraid to do, the stronger you'll become as a writer and as a human being.
- Learn to take a new risk in your writing every chance you get and call yourself a risk-writer.

SESSION 19

I Need a Drink/cigarette/Box of Chocolates, Right Now

"I never write when I'm drunk."
—W. H. Auden

One of the reasons some of you don't write is because you suffer from something called low frustration tolerance. Maybe you have a hard time dealing with frustrating situations or tasks, so you look for ways to avoid taking an action. In this case, that means you avoid writing.

How do you end up experiencing low frustration tolerance in your writing and in your life? Well, when you were very little you either learned about how to deal with frustration or you didn't. If you were raised in a home where you didn't get exactly what you wanted exactly when you wanted it, you eventually learned to develop what is called frustration tolerance. When you cried, you might have had to wait a little while before you were fed or picked up. In other words, your desires were frustrated. The greater the frustration you faced, the more tolerance you built up and you developed high frustration tolerance. On the other hand, you might have been raised in a home where your every wish was met immediately, in which case you experienced hardly any type of frustration. As a result, you developed very low frustration tolerance.

Were you one of those children who cried and got fed or picked up immediately? If you wanted a toy, did your parents get you one right away? Did you demand candy before dinner and get an entire box?

If this was the case, then you never learned how to deal or cope with frustration—thus, you never built up your frustration tolerance. You ended up wanting immediate gratification any time you were frustrated. This expectation extends to your writing and your creativity, too.

People with low frustration tolerance quit in the face of any difficulties or frustrations. Are you one of those people who quits rather than fights? Do you divert yourself with activities that provide immediate gratification instead of working through your frustrations? Do you escape your writing problems by going to the movies, talking on the phone, or watching television when you get blocked? You might eat, drink smoke, or shop so as not to deal with your writing frustrations and perhaps not even feel them.

This is especially true for those of you who have low frustration tolerance and want to become writers. This happens when you haven't developed your discipline muscles. The minute your writing doesn't work or your story is weak, you will most likely quit instead of working until you get your writing in shape. Your frustration tolerance is at too low a level.

Distracting yourself by watching films or television, eating or drinking, or shopping are ways of coping with your writing frustrations. These activities take no discipline or concentration, but they are very effective ways of relieving your anxiety about not writing. They temporarily distract you. You try to find other activities to alleviate your inner frustrations, and you stop writing at a time when it's most crucial for you to continue.

One of the most common ways of blocking your creativity is to give up too soon and not work through your writing obstacles. Lack of follow-through to complete your writing project stops your creativity because you can't handle frustration and aren't able to cope.

Don't run for cover when you feel frustrated in your writing. Be accountable, be still, and know that you won't die from psychic pain, loneliness, or fear. But your creative spirit will die if you don't give up your need for comfort foods, for sudden snacks, for brief binges, still the anxiety in yourself.

Look at the big picture with your writing and make it one of beauty and not grief, of joy and not despair, of fighting for your writing and not trying to ignore it. Through overeating and stuffing down feelings instead of dealing with them, all you're doing is numbing yourself and you'll eventually feel worse.

Develop the courage to feel your pain, feel your joy, and feel your creativity. When you are frustrated with your writing, you may avoid these feelings by running to alcohol, drugs, food, shopping, and other potentially harmful coping methods to calm the negative feelings inside of you. Believe it or not, you may also soothe yourself through oral gratification even when your creativity is actually flowing and flowing. You may wonder why this can happen when your writing is tumbling out. The reason is that you get so overwhelmed by the burst of creativity that you respond the same way that you do to frustration—by turning to a substance or activity that calms you down and relaxes you from your excitement.

Have faith, and believe that you can succeed in positive rather than harmful ways of coping with blocks and frustration. Compulsively obsessed behaviors are only a temporary means of escaping from and reducing inner turmoil and inner tensions. You can't develop coping mechanisms through your compulsive behavior—including shopping, drinking, smoking, sex, gambling, or eating. And when these behaviors are out of your control, they can become addictions.

Soon your means of coping to reduce anxiety becomes your biggest problem in your life. In other words, your solution to your writing frustration is now a larger problem than your original one. It is now a bigger problem than your low frustration tolerance. This starts a downward spiral and ends in feelings of low self-esteem, shame, anger, blame, and guilt. If you continue this pattern, you will subject yourself to more feelings of worthlessness, emptiness, and isolation. How in the world can you write under these circumstances? You can't.

A quick fix ends in a slow death of your dreams, of your hopes, and of your creative ability. Eventually, you make the situation worse. It's a vicious cycle that you need to stop before it stops you from realizing your dreams of becoming a writer.

The inability to take responsible actions when you're feeling frustrated prevents you from developing coping skills and healthy strategies. Giving in and giving up is not the answer. When you become frustrated in your writing, if you have the mistaken belief that writing should be easy, then you will use maladapted ways of coping.

You need to learn how to handle and deal with your writing frustration so you'll know how to tolerate it and write in spite of it. By feeling your frustration and not running away from it, you'll be able to increase your low frustration tolerance level in your writing as well as in your relationships and in your life.

On the Couch

"Things won are done, joy's soul lies in the doing."
—SHAKESPEARE

Kimberly was a young woman in her late twenties who was a freelance magazine writer. A very talented writer, she came to see me because lately she'd been depressed and having difficulty writing. She was also worried about her weight, having gained twenty pounds in the past three months.

She blamed her weight gain on the writing blocks she was experiencing. I asked her why she related not writing to her recent weight gain.

"I just want to eat when I'm blocked. Whenever I can't write, I need that cookie or cake when I get upset. It calms me. But lately I've been upset so much with my writing that I want to eat the minute I sit down at the computer."

"You want instant gratification. Is that how you coped with your frustration as a child?"

"I guess it is. When my parents would fight or I didn't want to do my home-work, I'd run to the refrigerator and eat or sneak cookies into my bedroom."

"Well, that's probably the pattern you developed to cope with stress and your distress. You never developed frustration tolerance, and immediate gratification was your solution."

We began working on her coping skills after she confessed that she always turned to food for every stressful occasion. Even when she felt good, as well as when she was depressed, sad, angry, tired, or frustrated, she turned to food. She'd go on eating binges when things really got bad, because she never learned how to develop good coping skills when upset or frustrated. Food was her coping mechanism. It worked until she started to gain a lot of weight, which upset her even more.

I suggested that she stop herself when she wanted to give up on the writing and to do something other than eat. "Get out of the house and take a walk when you're feeling the urge to eat over your writing frustration." Together we started to develop other strategies for her to use instead of eating, so that she would feel more in control and gain personal empowerment.

I said, "Write about your feelings of frustration the minute they arise. Write about your impulse to get immediate gratification through eating and how you try to soothe yourself with food. Wait a beat before you reach for food and count to twenty. Then continue to write about what you're feeling about yourself in the moment."

"I think I can handle that. I'm always writing in my journal."

"The more you give in to your cravings and impulses, the less you're able to cope with your creative blocks and your writing problems. And I'm sure you end up feeling desperate, guilty shameful, and isolated. There are many weight groups online or in town that you can join for support."

She promised to find a weigh support group like Weight Watchers or Overeaters Anonymous. "I need to be around people with a similar problem to mine.

"Just remember that you can develop self-discipline. This is a learned be-havior; you are the person who is in control of your life and your writing. It's up to you to get the outside support you need and to learn to develop self-control and self-discipline. You're not born with either, but you can develop them if you really want to write."

Off the Couch

"Great works are performed not by strength but by perseverance."
—SAMUEL JOHNSON

By her next visit Kimberly had found a support group that she liked. She still felt frustrated with her writing and continued to eat over it, but she was eating a little less than she had before joining the group.

"Kimberly, have you forgotten that writing isn't all about frustration. Instead of looking for instant gratification, write about what you're feeling even more than you did before. Just fight through your frustration."

"I try, but eating has always been such a comfort for me."

"Maybe it's time to get out of your comfort zone. When you become frustrated, write about it, but go even deeper. Write about your loneliness and the emptiness inside. And every time you stop yourself from eating, you'll just keep getting stronger and stronger on the inside."

Determined to become unblocked and write again, Kimberly followed my advice and started to build up her frustration tolerance. She stopped eating between meals and when she became frustrated with her writing, instead of turning to food, she went for a walk. The good news was that she started to lose weight because she wasn't running to food every time she met a roadblock in her writing or an obstacle with her creativity. She waited a "beat" before she reached for a cookie. Although this was a slow process, she worked on her coping skills and continued to write. Now she has gained balance in her life and in her writing because she has built up her frustration tolerance muscles and stopped responding out of the need for immediate gratification.

Shrink Rap

Wait a beat before you eat.
To keep on writing is a feat.
Wait a beat when there's too much heat.
To keep on writing can't be beat.

Creativity Chronicle

"Forming a new habit is like winding string on a ball."
—WILLIAM JAMES

Write about whether or not you have low frustration tolerance when coping with your writing and the ways you escape the frustration of being blocked. Write about how you can increase your frustration tolerance and how you can fight the easy self-gratification solutions, which are eventually the most difficult problems to solve.

SHRINK WRAP-UP: UNTIL NEXT TIME

- Learn to live with your writing frustration by flexing your writing muscles.
- Get out of your comfort zone when you're feeling anxious about writing and just write anyway.
- Don't give up on your writing too soon in the process. Stay the course.

SESSION 20

They Just Don't Get My Genius

"Genius is 1 percent inspiration and 99 percent perspiration."
—THOMAS A. EDISON

Denial is a simple defense mechanism that is used all the time. It prevents you from recognizing the uncomfortable reality of what is going on, especially when you are blocked. Denial allows you to ignore or deny experiences that increase your anxiety and that are too unpleasant for you to deal with. Denial in service of the ego is a powerful tool. It helps you get through life without feeling the pain of rejection, thus keeping your self-esteem intact. The motivation to use it is strong as denial does help you maintain your equilibrium and deal with the everyday frustrations you face.

However, denial taken to extremes can interfere with your ability to grow and mature as a writer and as a person. I've seen clients who are so into denial that they keep on sending out the same manuscript or script over and over again, never questioning whether the writing is working or not. They deny any constructive criticism and happily keep sending out their writing project without making the necessary changes to make the writing the best it can be.

I've also worked with writers whose denial served them well. Denial can be a way of pretending that your writing problems don't exist. So you don't give up, allowing you to work on your writing rather than spend time and energy dealing with your writing frustrations. It is only a good thing if your denial enables you to survive and keep on writing. Maybe your denial allows you to be persistent and keep on sending out your writing material, which also isn't a bad thing as long as you aren't having any problems with your writing.

Denial gets you in trouble when it keeps you from seeing the true flaws in your writing, things you really need to learn about and fix. Maybe your screenplay isn't in the right format, or maybe your characters are weak and the story just doesn't work. If you deny that there is anything wrong or that you need to go back and do some major rewrites, and you just keep on submitting your material, the only person you're kidding is yourself. Denial also can create psychological problems when you pretend that a painful event like getting rejected or criticized didn't happen, so that you don't recognize your disappointment as real. You're just fooling yourself instead of dealing with your true feelings about rejection.

Denying your writing frustrations or your blocked creativity and acting like things are great when everything is falling apart around you, is harmful to you in the long run. You're using denial of your reality as a way of avoiding something necessary, which is dealing with your pain, anxiety, and frustration. In this case, denial is a form of self-delusion and a way of indirectly hurting yourself. Unless you are able to deal with the reality of accepting criticism and the need to improve, you will fail—not only as a writer, but also as a person.

Even though your denial is a defense mechanism that may help you to cope, it often stops you from being all you can be in your creative life. For example, when you get rejected in your writing, you can deny it by putting your focus on a less painful event and refusing to accept the reality of your disappointment in getting rejected. Instead, you concentrate on something less important, like wanting to improve your tennis game. You spend the hours when you should be writing, out on the tennis court, hitting tennis balls for hours on end. In this case, you're not facing the objective reality of your writing life but living in denial.

A great example of denial is being on a diet and ordering apple pie á la mode and then requesting an artificial sweetener for your coffee. Haven't we all done this once or twice in our lives?

On the Couch

"Men have to find truth; not because it is lost but because they are lost."
—IVAN N. PANIN

Connie came to see me because she was blocked in her latest script and couldn't write. She told me that recently, she had not been asked to return to her job as a staff writer on an hour-long television drama, where she had worked as a writer for two years. As we spoke, she told me she and her husband were having problems, but that wasn't the reason she came to see me. She said that she was handling it. The real problem had to do with her not being able to write. After Connie had been in therapy with me for a couple of weeks, I said to her, "Maybe you're in denial."

She laughed as she replied, "How do you know if I'm in denial or I'm an optimist?"

"That's a great question." I thought about if for a minute to see if she was making a joke, but she was serious. "Well, one comes from weakness and the other from strength."

"What do you mean?" she asked.

"Whereas denial is used as a defense mechanism and comes from frustration, optimism comes from a positive attitude, self-esteem, and confidence in yourself and your writing. That is a major difference," I stated.

"Well, everything is really good except for my not writing."

She didn't want to do any writing exercises that I suggested, so we continued talking. But as she continued to be blocked, she was also more desperate. Staffing season was only weeks away and her agent wanted to send her out to meetings, but with more current material than her last credits.

Off the Couch

"Do we dare be ourselves? That is the question that counts."
—PABLO CASALS

I worked with Connie on changing her attitude and getting in touch with her real feelings. Finally, she was willing to do some writing about being in a bad relationship and getting fired from a writing job. In my office, she used my method to write about her relationship and getting fired from a writing job.

Once she began to write, she couldn't stop. As she read the words on the page, tears flowed down her cheeks. Here is what she wrote.

> "Beneath my smiling face I feel an unsettling gnawing inside of me. It's like free-floating sadness filling up my insides. I've always been able to pretend everything was okay with me. In fact, my friends always refer to me as easy-going and even-tempered. They didn't know that on the inside I feel bottled up, frustrated, and afraid. I hide my real feelings because that's how I've always been. But now I'm starting to feel as if I'll explode if I don't get them out. I've always denied anything that upset me all of my life. I've been so good at that until now. I don't know what I'm really feeling anymore or if what I feel is real or made up by me. I just know that whatever I've been denying all my life isn't working for me now. I'm a mess inside and out. I just know it feels awful not to be writing and not to be working. I'm scared I'll never work again and I'm terrified that I can't hold on to my relationship, which is being affected by my scared self. I don't know what to do anymore or even how to do it. I feel lost."

When she read what she'd written, she started to sob. "You're right, I just didn't want to face the problems in my relationship, and I'm afraid it's falling apart. As for writing...I may never get another job. I know I was so preoccupied with my disintegrating relationship that I couldn't contribute to the show like I used to."

This was a huge breakthrough in Connie's therapy. She stopped living in denial and started to face the reality of her life. She also stopped pretending everything was exactly how she wanted it and began facing her truth. Even though it was a painful process, once she was aware of how she had been denying the problems in her relationship and putting her fears on her writing, she was able to take the first step in overcoming her problems by dealing with them and making new choices.

Connie's now writing again, and she and her husband are trying to resolve issues in their marriage through marital counseling. Since Connie stopped using denial as a defense, she is dealing with not protecting herself from the reality of her relationship problems. She faced the fact that she was blaming everything on not writing, when in fact she got writer's block because of her denial of her painful emotions regarding her marriage.

Shrink Rap

I faced myself and found my fears, hidden in a pool of tears. I faced my fears and found myself, and now I'm free to express the real me.

Creativity Chronicle

"The deepest principle of human nature is the craving to be appreciated."
—WILLIAM JAMES

Using Ballon Method Writing™ write about a time you used denial to protect yourself from frustration or painful feelings with your blocked creativity. Become aware of yourself in relationship to your denial and write about how you can transform it into acceptance of the objective reality of your writing and your life. Be realistic.

SHRINK WRAP-UP: UNTIL NEXT TIME

- Don't be afraid to face your reality in your writing.
- Denial helps you in the short run, but using denial hurts you in the long haul.
- Feel your frustration and your writing anxiety without denying them.

SESSION 21

My Father Was Right!

*"It is the tension between creativity and skepticism
that has produced the stunning and unexpected."*
—CARL SAGAN

Was your father right about you when he told you that your writing was stupid? Was your piano teacher right about you when he shouted that you were tone deaf? Was your grandmother right on target when she told you that you were too loud?

These are some of the beliefs you could have been given from family, teachers, or peers. They are called self-defeating beliefs because they hold you back in your work and in your life. They may be true but most likely are not.

If your beliefs don't cause you any problems and you're able to achieve what you want, then you have no problems. The self-defeating beliefs that are dangerous are the ones you carry inside you without ever realizing it. These are often the culprits for procrastination, creative blocks, and a negative frame of mind. In general, self-defeating beliefs are the ones that create writing problems for you that are ultimately self-destructive.

Are you often late for your deadline? Do you have problems with putting your emotions in your writing? Do you become too unfocused when you are writing and end up writing drivel? Do you try to write perfectly and get depressed when you can't?

These are just some harmful behaviors that are instigated by your self-defeating beliefs, which are sabotaging you and your writing success. Unfortunately, they have power over your thoughts, feelings, and behavior. They are negative because you're not even aware of them. They stop you from being all you can be and doing all you can do with your creativity. The only way to overcome them is to first become aware that they exist.

Self-defeating beliefs are what you often determine as facts, when in reality they are just beliefs. Most likely, these beliefs were given to you as a small child and have remained in your unconscious. They often pull invisible strings that cause you to be blocked in your creative ideas and stuck in your writing, while at the same time causing you to doubt yourself.

Stop listening to these self-defeating beliefs and identify them. This way you can at least start the process of bringing them to your awareness and eventually refute them. Until you do, they'll remain an intransigent as a bad habit and prevent you from reaching your writing goals.

These beliefs are insidious and enslaving, poisonous and powerful. What you believe about yourself and your writing can make you feel insecure, unsure, stuck, afraid, and unsuccessful. You need to look at how your self-defeating beliefs are limiting your writing and your creative life and reframe them. All of your irrational beliefs can create your fears. They damage your self-esteem and cripple your spirit. It's up to you to give yourself a reality check to decide if they're irrational and illogical. Most likely they are.

In all my years as a writing therapist and consultant, one of the main things I have discovered is this: You can't go beyond or reach more than what your beliefs say you can. What does this mean?

It means that you need to examine your existing beliefs and see how they hold you back in your writing and also in your life. You must change your self-defeating beliefs because you can never exceed them.

Are you a poor risk-taker in your writing? Do you get easily depressed and fearful when your writing is rejected? Are you thin-skinned and easily discouraged when your writing is criticized? If your answer to most of these questions is yes, you need to take an inventory of your belief system.

Is your creative garden filled with flowers or overrun with the weed of self-destructive beliefs? Tend your creative garden. Weed out these beliefs, while letting your creativity bloom with ideas, poetry, music, art, and writing.

On the Couch

"Writing is a form of therapy."
—GRAHAM GREENE

Ed was a professional nonfiction writer who had written two books in the field of psychology, but he wasn't happy with either. He had a contract to write his third book and came to see me because he was in a deep funk, unable to write.

"The voice that criticizes me—it hates me. It has a powerful energy, and I'm aware that I've created that energy myself."

"Why do you think you're blocked now, especially when you have a contract and received an advance? You certainly don't have to worry about the book not being published."

"I know, but my books just haven't done that well. So maybe I'm just cynical with this one."

"What do you mean by cynical?" I asked.

"My critical voice tells me, 'Why bother? None of your other books sold well. All this writing is just for pennies.' I keep hearing that voice and its power stops me in the middle of my writing."

"Do you want to give the advance back and not fulfill your contract?"

Ed became very indignant. "Heck no? I'm here to get unblocked so I can finish the book."

"Well, at least you know that you're not just motivated by your royalties and you want to write the book. Right?"

"So why am I not writing? Am I punishing myself?"

As we explored Ed's resistance to writing, I asked him to write down all of his self-defeating beliefs that keep him stuck and not writing. He wrote down quite a few, which he identified as coming from something he called "The Vicious Voice":

"Why don't you get a real job?"
"Look who thinks he's a writer."
"You're not the type to be a writer."
"Writing is a waste of your time."

As he read them, he was surprised at how powerful they were.

"I think I know who the voice is that tells me I'm a fraud, not good enough, and a failure."

"Who is it?"

"The voice is the voice of my own self-hatred."

"I believe our work is cut out for us. Now that you are aware of your self-defeating beliefs, you'll be able to change them or at the very least discover their origin."

Off the Couch

"The good writing of any age has always been the product of someone's neurosis."
—WILLIAM STYRON

As Ed continued to refute his self-defeating beliefs, he became less blocked. "I'm fighting back against that Vicious Voice, which really was the voice of my father. He'd always put me down because I didn't like sports, but loved music, art, and writing."

"I'm sure that hurt you, but it's interesting that you've had the courage to pursue your creativity, rather than acquiesce to negative beliefs you were told."

Ed smiled and looked proud. In a short time, he not only was able to disagree with the Vicious Voice, but he no longer bought into what it said.

One of the positive things he wrote against the Vicious Voice was as follows: "You're wrong, and I don't have to prove anything to you. I love writing!"

The simple act of writing new dialogue enabled Ed to stand up to his father regarding his writing. In forming new beliefs, he experienced himself in a new way, which made his creativity more available to him for his writing. He finally experienced a freedom from the Vicious Voice, which had always depleted his creative energy with its constant predictions of failure.

After transforming his self-defeating beliefs into self-affirming beliefs, Ed achieved greater confidence and more awareness of his writing talent. He was no longer depressed or blocked.

Ed said, "I'm now not ashamed of being a writer, since I got rid of my self-defeating beliefs."

Shrink Rap

Vicious Voice: *"You can't write a complete sentence."*
Nurturing Voice: *"You're an imaginative writer."*
Vicious Voice: *"Your writing is stilted."*
Nurturing voice: *"Your writing is interesting and deep."*

Creativity Chronicle

"I want it said of me by those who knew me best, that I always plucked a thistle and planted a flower where I thought a flower would grow."
—ABRAHAM LINCOLN

Write down all your self-defeating and irrational beliefs, and describe how they limit your writing and your life. Next, write about letting go of your self-defeating beliefs and changing them to self-affirming beliefs and how you feel. Read them over every day and night for twenty-one days (the time it takes you to learn something new). Be certain to use Ballon Method Writing.™

SHRINK WRAP-UP: UNTIL NEXT TIME

- By changing your self-defeating beliefs you'll improve your writing.
- Write even though your irrational beliefs try to hold you back.
- Remember you can't exceed your beliefs about yourself as a writer, so believe that you'll succeed.

SESSION 22

Oops, I May Not Have a Climax!

"Books are never finished, they are merely abandoned."
—OSCAR WILDE

Some people keep dozens of different writing projects going at the same time. When it's time to finish the first one, off they go to start work on the next. Nothing is ever finished. It's a vicious cycle you may develop with your writing, and it leads nowhere. Hopping from one project to another without finishing any of them keeps you going in circles: the end result is that you just get too dizzy to finish anything you write.

Fear of finishing, fear of the unknown, fear of failure, and fear of rejection are just some of the reasons writers never complete their work. Many writers suddenly come up with new ideas for completely different projects when their current project is stuck in the second act, the main character is a bore, or they can't create conflict. You can't succeed or fail if you don't ever finish what you're writing, can you?

However, there are other basic reasons for not finishing your writing that have to do with craft. Do you say you're blocked when in actuality you don't know how to structure or outline a project? Not finishing often has more to do with lack of craft than it does with being blocked. I can't begin to tell you how many people start writing without the slightest idea of the rules governing good writing, character development, and solid story structure. Can you believe that people actually begin a screenplay without learning anything about dramaturgy? Well, it's true. After teaching thousands of writers—from beginners to professionals—how to create a blueprint from idea to completed script or manuscript—I'm amazed at how few writers have paid attention to craft.

Are you a writer who keeps getting bogged down in the middle of your plot and who doesn't know what to do next? Or do you have trouble not knowing the ending of your story, so that you can't finish? Do you write without any idea where you're going after the first chapter or the first page or the first word? If your answer to the above questions is yes, you should probably take a writing course, study writing books or screenplays, and read a lot of material in the genre in which you want to write.

If your creativity is easily accessible to you then you probably have a lot of wonderful ideas, but writing is really about taking your ideas and putting them into a solid story structure with complex, interesting characters who have depth. This takes hard work, discipline, dedication, and perseverance if you want to complete your writing.

On the Couch

"You can't test courage cautiously."
—ANNE DILLARD

A couple of years ago, an older woman came to see me with bundles and scraps of unfinished novels, short stories, and fragments of ideas for a poetry book. She almost literally had tons of papers that she kept shuffling around while she spoke to me. I listened as she told me her story of always wanting to be a writer and how she'd jotted down her ideas, thoughts, and snippets of stories, but never put them into a format or a form to write.

"I want you to help me get some of these story ideas into shape so that I can start working on them and send them out."

I looked them over and managed to help her choose a couple of her favorites from all the torn bits of papers and old notebooks she had. It was a formidable task and she was overwhelmed by all the scraps of notes she had. I was, too.

"Okay, your assignment is to finish this short story that you've worked on for years but never completed," I said.

She looked relieved and thanked me for my help in guiding her on how to finish one of her stories. We set up an appointment for two weeks and she was excited when she left.

"Thank you so much. I'm going home right now to finish my story."

Two weeks later she didn't show up for her appointment. I called, thinking she might have forgotten. Saddened, I learned that she had a heart attack. A few weeks later I read her obituary in the paper, where it was noted that she had always loved writing.

What's the point of the story? Well, it's that time isn't open-ended and you need to have the courage to finish what you start. At least make completing something your creative goal. Otherwise, you're only wasting your creative energy and your time. It's important to get what you have written out into the universe, to respect your hard work, and to acknowledge that you have something important to write.

I often think of that lovely woman and feel sorry she never realized her writing dreams. Don't let your creativity be something you'll end up regretting, because you didn't complete your writing. Do it now and finish it. Be persistent not resistant.

Off the Couch

"When we face our fears and let ourselves know our connection to the power that is in us and beyond us, we learn courage."
—ANNE WILSON SCHARF

Mike, a man in his middle forties, was another writer who had a similar problem of not being able to finish anything he started. He came into my office with notebooks and papers sticking out of them, like so many other writers who never finish their projects. He wanted to work with me because he had read my book and wanted to complete all the writing projects he'd started.

"Any suggestions for people who get incredibly excited about a new idea every time they're working on something else?" Mike asked. "I always seem to come up with a great new project that obsesses me while I'm trying to finish the first one, and I don't know why."

"Do you think you have a fear of completing your writing? Then it would no longer be in your control."

"I don't know. But I have so many writing projects I need you to help me decide what to write first and then how to get them into shape."

"You certainly aren't alone in not completing what you write. There could be a myriad of reasons, but let's focus on choosing three projects you want to finish the most and start working on them."

Mike returned with a list of his top three projects. I worked with him on the first, and it really was a wonderful story. I was excited for him because he was a terrific writer. The very next session, when I was waiting to hear him read his completed short story, he began to read an entirely different one.

"What happened, Mike? I thought you were going to finish the short story you had chosen."

"I just decided I liked this one better."

This happened again even though he'd told me he wanted to complete his projects. I finally pointed out to him that his behavior illustrated he wasn't ever going to finish anything unless he found the reason he went from project to project. His frustration with himself was evident when he asked me why he still didn't stay with one project.

"I'm not sure. Maybe you don't like what you've written or you're tired of the subject or bored with the story. Then again, maybe the work is too hard and you're not finishing so you won't fail or be criticized.

"I'm not afraid of anyone judging me. I can handle it." He obviously was very frustrated with himself.

"Mike, what happens when you have to work hard and fight to make your story work?"

He thought for a minute. "I don't like to tackle the writing problems. I just want my writing to flow and when it doesn't I move on to the next."

"There you have it, Mike! You don't finish because you aren't willing to work hard. It takes discipline to constantly challenge your writing to be the best it can be."

"I never thought about the connection between not finishing and lack of discipline."

"It seems as if you don't like to have structure not only in your writing, but also in your life."

"You're right. I'm a spontaneous kind of guy and don't like spending too much time or effort on anything, including writing."

"You'll never succeed if you don't accept that it takes discipline, persistence, and hard work to finish your writing project. You need to make a commitment to work hard to reach 'The End.'"

Mike soon changed his attitude and made a commitment to work on his current writing project until he finished it. And he actually did finish it and some of his favorite other projects. He gained confidence in his writing ability as he successfully completed his unfinished projects.

At our last session he said, "Through my work with you I've learned how to discipline myself, set up a schedule, and write on a daily basis. I'm amazed at how much I've accomplished by sticking to one project. I won't stop working on the screenplay I started until I reach the climax and work out the resolution!"

Shrink rap

Don't give up in your writing. Stick to it and stick it out. Be persistent and not resistant. That's what writing is all about.

Creativity Chronicle

"The great thing in the world is not so much where we are
but in what direction we are going."
—OLIVER WENDELL HOLMES

If you are having difficulty finishing your writing projects, you need to write about it. Delve into the reasons such as fear of failure or fear of rejection, to discover if there are other reasons you aren't finishing. You'll feel like a real writer when you honor your writing by completing it.

SHRINK WRAP-UP: UNTIL NEXT TIME

- Commit yourself to one writing project and complete it before starting the next one.
- Have respect for yourself and for your writing by finishing it.
- Don't be a writer who regrets not finishing anything. No regrets, please.

SESSION 23

There's a Comma Missing on Page 329

"If you have the courage to begin, you have the courage to succeed."
—David Viscott

When I teach my workshops, the first thing I tell the students is that there will be no destructive criticism in the class. I will only tolerate *constructive* criticism. That means unless they have a positive way to give criticism, without hurting or embarrassing another writer, they should not say anything at all.

Constructive criticism is encouraging. It gives specific feedback, which a writer may or may not choose to take, and remains focused on the writing. In other words, in order to instill a safe environment for writers to feel protected and creative, these are the rules. Nobody in any of my classes is allowed to attack the writing, the writer, or make value judgments as to the merit of the subject matter.

The most consistent comment I get from my students is, "Thank you for creating such a safe writing environment. I really appreciated it."

A safe writing atmosphere is the only kind that you need to have in order to release your creativity through your writing. Many clients who have come to see me privately were blocked by another person's thoughtless or destructive criticism.

Remember, writers tend to have fragile egos. It's a shame that there are so many writing teachers and writing groups that do not make it their top priority to allow you to feel safe and supported. I can't begin to tell you the number of writers who have been deeply blocked for long periods of time because of a teacher's sarcasm about their writing or by having to listen to students in a class actually tear their writing apart without offering any constructive advice.

One client told me about an online novel-writing course she had taken. She received feedback from an e-mail the instructor wrote, "My favorite page was 136, because it was blank." And then he put the symbol of a smiling face beside his insulting remark. I guess he thought by showing a smiling face that he'd absolve himself from making such a stupid criticism. Well, if he was joking, it was a cruel joke. She was not only blocked, she'd lost all confidence in her fiction writing and hadn't picked up her novel in over a year, until she came to see me. It's amazing that such an insensitive individual could be in the position of teaching writing. Another client told me that his creative writing teacher was the only one during his graduate school career to ever give him a C. "The writing style she liked was William Faulkner, and I write more like Ernest Hemingway. Maybe I should have changed my style to suit her, but I never did and she never was open enough not to prejudge." In this case my client could never, ever please the teacher because his writing style was not to her liking. Yet he had the courage to write with his voice and not change it to write for a grade.

It's difficult not to write for a teacher or a group. I call that writing for consensus, especially if teachers are too subjective and narrow in their thinking. This happens more often than not, so be aware when you take a writing class or join a writers' group to enter at your own risk. I kid you not. Do your homework before you take a class or join a group and get feedback from other writers about the instructor if you can.

If a teacher is sarcastic, insensitive, or ridicules your writing, *run*—don't walk—to the nearest door and ask for your money back. If you're in a group of writers in which you are put down and given destructive criticism, you need to get out of the group. Better yet, have a set of ground rules for everyone in advance to be sure that the critique of your work is provided in a positive way.

That means if you think something should be changed or removed, you should give and be given concrete criticism that is specific and helpful. Don't let anyone say, "I don't like that idea," or "I don't like your writing," or "Your character is stupid." These comments are neither helpful nor productive. They're just mean and destructive. And the only thing they achieve is to block you and belittle you.

What happens to you when your writing is criticized? Do you stop writing? Does your creativity evaporate? Does your motivation cease? Do you feel just awful about yourself and your writing?

Look at your writing objectively and make the final decision of whether or not you want to accept others' criticism. Digest it and take what you want, if anything, and then let the rest go. Trust your creative instincts and your gut feelings.

I've worked with many writers who have been criticized, embarrassed, and humiliated. As a result, many of them not only became blocked, they were also insecure and unsure of whether they wanted to continue to write. They were deeply hurt writers on the inside and walking-wounded writers on the outside—the fallout from having been made fun of, insulted, or put down in regard to their writing.

This is what happened to Lisa, a writer who had been blocked for years when she came to see me.

On the Couch

"It is easy to be brave from a safe distance."
—Aesop

Lisa loved writing, but she hadn't written for years. In her late thirties, Lisa had been an avid writer before two painful incidents occurred when she was still writing.

The first situation happened while she was taking a writing workshop in the extension writer's program at one of the local universities. "We had to turn in our weekly assignments. When my teacher read what I had written, she embarrassed me in front of the entire class. 'What is this about? It doesn't make any sense.' She told me. I was so embarrassed I wanted to die.

"Well, that certainly was cruel and very insensitive. What happened next?" I asked.

"I never said anything because she was so opinionated, but that was the last time I went to class. There was no point in discussing it with her, and the sting of her words wounded my insides."

"Her comments were totally inappropriate. It's too bad so many colleges hire people who have writing credits but poor teaching skills," I told her.

"I was too defeated to try another class so I decided to join a writers' group with other writers. We all were writers of about equal ability and none of us were professionals. We met every week at a person's home and it seemed like a safe place. After a few weeks it was my turn to read. By the time they finished criticizing me, I didn't even remember what I had written. They had changed my story so much, they acted as if it was *their* story.

I had heard different versions of the same tale. So many blocked writers, who came to see me, had become blocked from writing classes and groups where they were given destructive criticism or just were humiliated by an insensitive writing teacher.

It's too bad they didn't deal with the story you'd written rather than just talk about how they would have liked it to be."

"I thought maybe I'd give it a try and take their advice. Well, the next time I read the changes I had made, according to their suggestions. And they didn't like the story that way, either! They told me one thing, and the very next week they asked why I made those changes. This happened week after week until I came to see you. I don't even know what my story is about anymore."

"That's a common problem—knowing when to keep your story and not to lose your vision, yet being able to make changes when it is necessary."

It was clear Lisa's confidence was almost nonexistent and she was feeling fragile about her writing ability.

"Lisa, you're suffering the fallout from writers' groups filled with people who spend so much time wanting to be brilliant in their criticisms that they do more damage than good."

We needed to work together so that I could help Lisa regain her confidence and start to write again.

Off the Couch

"I wrote because I had to. I couldn't stop. There wasn't anything else I could do."
—TENNESSEE WILLIAMS

I planned Lisa's session to help her get to the bottom of why she let other people—teachers and writers included—affect her so much that she became blocked. Much of our work together was to help her discover how she could start writing again, but it was also intended to help her develop strategies so she wouldn't become blocked every time she was criticized.

"Do you think you're a people pleaser, always wanting to please others instead of yourself?"

"Oh, am I ever! That's been my biggest problem, because I'm always worried about whether or not other people like me."

"Well, guess what, Lisa? You're also a 'writer pleaser.'"

"What do you mean by that?"

"Do you write to please others?"

She thought for a while and said, "Yes, I guess I am a 'writer pleaser.' I don't like it when others aren't happy with my writing."

It turned out that Lisa's creative block had a lot more to do with her *reaction* to the criticism she received. Her block was now understandable, since she had put her self-worth and value as a writer and a person on the opinions of other people.

We worked on helping her to become less and less of a people pleaser in her life, so that she could stop being a "writer pleaser" in her writing life.

I told her, "Don't let other individuals' opinions of your writing define your writing or you as a writer. And don't allow yourself to be affected by their criticisms to the point that you stop writing."

"Since I've been working on myself, I don't need to be as much of a people or writer pleaser as I used to be."

"Remember criticism is subjective and can be influenced by another person's mood, frame of mind, or self-esteem. Be professional and see if the criticism is meaningful or helpful. If not, don't be defensive. All you need to say is, 'That's interesting. I'll have to think about it.' Trust yourself and write on."

Lisa isn't blocked anymore, now that she has gained more insight into herself as a person and as a writer. She now concentrates on pleasing herself because she's now writing what she loves.

Shrink Rap

Stop being a people pleaser and a writer pleaser, too.
Write for yourself and from yourself, and you'll find your dreams come true.

Creativity Chronicle

"In writing and politicking, it is best not to think about it, just do it."
—GORE VIDAL

Recall a time when you read something you wrote and were criticized, embarrassed or judged. Write about how you felt with that destructive criticism. Are you still being influenced by that situation? Are you a "Writer pleaser"? If yes, write about it and how you need to stop writing to please others and learn to please yourself.

SHRINK WRAP-UP: UNTIL NEXT TIME

- Constructive criticism is the only kind to listen to.
- Join a writing class or writing group and make sure it's a safe and positive environment.
- Stop being a "writer pleaser" and write to please yourself.

SESSION 24

Conquering Page Fright

"He who is not every day conquering some fear has not learned the secret of life."
—RALPH WALDO EMERSON

Page fright is the writer's equivalent of stage fright—the feeling of freezing up when faced with a blank page. It can be an anxiety-provoking situation for many writers. If you have page fright, you might be lucky enough to be one of those writers whose anxiety goes away just as soon as you begin to write.

For other writers, page fright is actually a variation on performance anxiety, which manifests itself as page fright because of internal reasons. Others of you may have page fright because you really could be suffering from writing apprehension, lack of self-confidence, or fear.

There are many reasons for performance anxiety, which can happen not just with writing or other kinds of artistic performance but in almost every kind of life situation, from making a free throw in basketball when the score is tied and the clock is running out, to satisfying your mate when having sex.

Are you afraid of the empty page, just like actors are terrified of the empty stage? Are you afraid of the unknown when you stare at the empty page or computer screen that is filled with large empty white space? What about the empty yellow pad just waiting to be filled up? Does this vast emptiness frighten or stop you in your tracks?

To be creative, you need to have the courage to jump into the void of the empty page and create something out of nothing. Many successful and famous actors have had stage fright throughout their careers. Not just once or twice, but every time they are about to go on stage. Some throw up, others need a drink, and others need to be alone. But after they go on stage, something magical happens and their acting is brilliant.

Well, the same experience is often true for professional writers who have written best-selling books and award-winning screenplays. Every new writing project is just like starting from scratch.

One such famous novelist who was blocked told me, "Sometimes, I forget that I've published five novels. I'm stuck again, and it never gets easier when I start a new one. I even try to remember what I did in the last novel because I go through this block whenever I start a new book."

It is quite logical to have page fright. Don't feel guilty about being afraid of the blank page. Don't think you aren't a writer if you don't rush to the computer first thing when you get up in the morning in order to face the empty page. Writing is hard work. Filing up an empty page with your thoughts, your pains, your joys, and your creative ideas takes immense courage. You may become anxious every time you have to look at the empty page. Writing is hard work. Filling up an empty page with your thoughts, your pains, your joys, and your creative ideas takes immense courage. You may become anxious every time you have to look at the empty page and know you need to fill it up with dynamic dialogue, colorful characters, and clear, concise writing.

You may ask yourself any of these questions:

"Can I write this?"
'Will it be great?"
"Will I have something worthwhile to write?"
"Does it matter?"

All of the above questions can and do create anxiety inside you. They are based on your ego, or your lack of ego, a belief in yourself and your writing ability. The problem is you're not concentrating on the process or the joy of writing because you're too busy judging yourself. It's important for you to reclaim your love of writing and not focus on how good your writing is.

On the Couch

"He who fears something gives it power over him."
—MOORISH PROVERB

Barbara, a competent woman in her early forties, was a writer of young adult novels. She had been a consistent writer until she suddenly developed page fright. She was suffering from major anxiety and fear of the blank page and would stare at the computer screen for hours on end without writing.

Although she had two prior published books and was a diligent worker, she now was having nothing but blocks with her third book. Her deadline was growing closer, and she hadn't even completed a first draft when she came to see me.

"I love to write, but the problem is I have a terrible, awful, difficult time facing the empty page. I actually get the shakes and become completely immobilized."

"But you have already written two books that have been published, so what do you think it is about the empty page that frightens you now?"

"I wish I knew. And what makes this situation so strange and hard for me to figure out is that once I finally do break through the fear and begin writing. I love it! And yet, the very next day, I go through the whole process again. My mind knows that once I start, I will enjoy the process immensely, yet I don't know how to convince my mind to skip over that initial immobilizing fear of putting words on the blank page."

At first I gave Barbara simple techniques that had worked for other writers, such as listening to relaxing music before writing. Another technique I have her was to meditate for fifteen minutes before she was to begin writing. This helped her relax and get into an "alpha" state where she was one with the empty page. I even suggested using stickers.

"Why don't you go out and buy different stickers. Pick your favorites such as hearts, flowers, happy faces, and so on. Put them on the empty pages of your Creativity Chronicle, and they'll be inviting to you when you begin to write. Your focus won't be so much on the emptiness of the page, because it will be filled with colorful figures."

The following week she returned and had stickers on every page of her chronicle. "I love the stickers looking back at me, especially the smiley faces. It does help me, but I'm still having the same problem with my anxiety."

It was time to work on Barbara and the real source of her anxiety. I could see that techniques and simple strategies wouldn't solve her real problem, which appeared to be internal.

"I want you to write out all the fears you have when facing the empty page."

"But I came to see you with help on writing my book."

"We are going to help you with your book by first doing this exercise. Remember to write down all of your fears when you sit down to write."

Barbara returned the following week with her list of fears. Not surprisingly, she had written pages. I had her circle the most powerful of all the fears she had listed:

"I'll never have another successful book like my first one."
"They'll find out that I'm writing the same book over again."
"I resent having other people judge my writing."
"I'm sick and tired of having to fill the page with a brilliant story."

After hearing all of her fears, I told her that I could see how difficult it has been for her to encounter all of them every single time she sat down to write. "It must be exhausting."

She agreed that writing had become a chore rather than the creative challenge it used to be. As we continued to work to identify Barbara's fears and talk about them in therapy, she began to recognize the basic problem related to her page fright.

"I guess I've really never been able to truly believe in myself. I've always had to work doubly hard for everything I've ever attained in my writing life, or for that matter in any part of my life."

"Why don't you think you've never believed in yourself?"

"The easy answer would be because my parents didn't want me to become a writer. They wanted me to be a teacher."

"Maybe there are other reasons you haven't believed in yourself."

"You're probably right; I think it's something deeper than the obvious reason."

Off the Couch

"The best way out is always through."
—ROBERT FROST

As we worked together, Barbara began to realize that her lack of belief in herself came from a very deep place within. "I put on a good front and everyone thinks I'm capable and confident, but in truth I'm scared."

"Let's find out where this started." I gave Barbara the assignment to write about a time when she had done something creative as a child and suddenly became afraid.

The following week Barbara returned with her Ballon Method Writing™ assignment and couldn't wait to read it.

"I am so proud of being in a piano recital at my school. I am nine years old and wearing my prettiest pink party dress and I'm playing "Für Elise." I have memorized the piece and know it perfectly, but suddenly for only a minute I go blank. My hands start to shake and it seems like hours, but soon I start to play again. Over the music I hear laughter from the audience. I can't understand who's laughing and why. I am upset and hurt as I look and it's my dad.

My own dad is sitting in the first row laughing in front of all the parents and teachers and kids. I want to die. It's just a big joke to him but to me it is humiliating. Why is he laughing? Why is he making fun of his own daughter? I run off the stage to the sound of applause, but I know it's not real. My father's laughter is the only real truth for me."

Barbara stopped reading and was shaking, her face pale. "I can't believe this is still so painful to me after all these years."

"These hurtful memories are tucked away in our unconscious and provide the fuel for your page fright and other creative blocks," I said.

As we continued probing memories she said, "I remember other times he made fun of me. I know he probably wasn't deliberately being mean but just acting like a big kid where everything's a joke. I just can't believe that it's these memories of my father that has been what's stopping me. I thought his ridicule didn't bother me anymore, but it still does."

"Now that you've recalled these painful memories, which are the basis of your performance anxiety you'll be able to fight and eventually overcome them," I said.

Through Barbara's writing, we worked together on her unfinished business with her father's cavalier attitude towards her. Eventually, she worked through it by realizing that his actions weren't really about her but that the real problem had to do with him.

By working on past experiences and insensitive situations regarding herself and her father, Barbara now has a firm belief in herself and in her writing. She no longer has page fright.

Shrink Rap

Creating something out of nothing is exciting. Filling the empty page with words, sacred words, is inviting.

Creative Chronicle

"The creation of a thousand forests is in on acorn."
—RALPH WALDO EMERSON

When you feel frightened of the empty page, write a list of all your worries and fears. Read over the list after it's completed and see if you can identify a more specific problem related to your list. Write about a time when you were creative and someone embarrassed you so that you stopped feeling positive about your creative abilities. Change the story and rewrite it about how you can now forget that situation and move on as a courageous, creative writer.

SHRINK WRAP-UP: UNTIL NEXT TIME

- Buy some colorful stickers and put them on the empty page of your Creativity Chronicle to make the blank pages more friendly and inviting.
- Read your favorite poetry for twenty minutes and get into the rhythm of the words before you sit down to write.
- Make friends with the blank page by listening to relaxing music before writing.

SESSION 25

Motivate Thyself

"Writing is an exploration. You start from nothing and learn as you go."
—E. L. DOCTOROW

To be a productive writer, you must have inner motivation. As a creative writer you also need to have a sense of your own power. Otherwise, you will stop writing the first time you are rejected. This means your motivation to be a writer must come from within you, not because other people have told you that you should write.

I've heard so many individuals say, "My relatives tell me I should write my story," or "I was told I have writing talent," or "My girlfriend said I write a terrific letter," or "Boy, you should hear about some stories I have to tell."

This is all well and good, except that to be a successful writer, motivation needs to come from you. It's an inside job. Although the above reasons for writing might be flattering and ego rewarding, they aren't enough of a reason to write. To be a writer, you must be willing to learn the craft and pay your dues because you *love* writing and want to write something about which you're passionate, no matter what happens!

If you are motivated to be a writer, not because of what others have told you but because of your burning desire to write, then you're on the right path as you undertake your writing journey.

True motivation doesn't come from other people. External motivation usually doesn't last for too long when you want to write. If you're only motivated to write because you want to please other people or impress them, you should quit now. Writing is not only too hard, but you'll also stop the first time you get criticized. Write out of love for the craft and you'll stay with it.

Another reason motivation needs to come from within is that it helps you set your own goals as a writer. By setting writing goals and reaching them, you are motivating yourself every day. The more you feel good about your writing plan, the better motivated you'll become. There's no freedom without personal responsibility.

Writing for a sustained period of time, like the year or more it might very well take you to complete a novel or screenplay, is impossible without your own inner motivation. Inner motivation is what gives you the energy to be persistent and to persevere when you feel frustrated and blocked in your creative efforts and want to give up. It's your inner motivation that is caused by your joy in the writing process and your love of the work. Your desire to write must come from your intrinsic motivation, not because of other people or because you're motivated by outside forces such as wanting money or fame.

Although these external rewards are the reasons that a lot of writers write, they aren't strong enough motivations to keep you writing when you're rejected or become frustrated in the writing process. Those reasons will fade into nothing like dust in the wind the first time you become conflicted or anxious with your writing. I've discovered that more than talent, it is a writer's inner motivation or drive that is most important in the creative process when it comes to the ability and drive to continue writing. It's your inner motivation that helps you maintain a strong desire and concrete goals, which in turn make you persevere in the face of creative blocks or writing frustrations.

On the Couch

"The abundant life does not come to those who have had a lot of obstacles removed from their path by others. It develops from within and is rooted in strong mental and moral fiber."
—WILLIAM MATHER LEWIS

"How can you motivate yourself to create the writing life you need in order to be more successful?"

"I don't know," Paul answered. He was a novelist who had one novel published and was so unmotivated that he couldn't continue to work on writing his second, although he was halfway through. I could feel his frustration, which showed on his face.

"You know that to be motivated as a writer you must have passion, enthusiasm, and the courage to take risks in your writing."

"I try to keep being motivated, but I can't seem to sustain it. I start worrying if my novel is worth writing and if it'll be published."

"You need to write because of *you* and not because of outside influences. Your motivation has to come from the inside out. Your desire, dreams, and dedication must be the things that keep you going."

"Easier said than done," Paul responded.

"Actually, it's easier done than said," I replied. "Do you have a belief in your writing and in yourself as a writer?"

"I think I do, but then I start worrying if anyone will like my novel. Soon I start feeling really low, and my motivation seems to disappear."

Off the Couch

"It is by sitting down to write every morning that one becomes a writer."
—GERALD BRENON

Paul's problem is one that many experienced writers face: How you keep motivated on a long-term project like a novel, a nonfiction book, or a screenplay when you don't know whether all of your hard work will pay off? Will you reach the goals you have set for your writing? Will your writing sell, be published or produced? Will you get paid? Become famous? Make money?

As I told Paul, "In order to succeed as a writer, you need to take pleasure in your writing and in the writing process, no matter how difficult you find it to be. Don't look for external motivation to keep you going because it won't."

As a writer who had already enjoyed success with his earlier publications, Paul needed to understand those forces inside that motivated his behavior to write in the first place.

"I want you to do the following assignment about your motivation to write. Answer the question, 'Why Do I Write?' and see if you can reconnect to your original muse.

The next session he read what he had written, titled "Why I Write":

"I write for the same reason I breathe. I have to. I write to stay alive. I write to take stock of who I am and what I'm really feeling without being told by others what I should feel and how I should feel. I write to feel connected to my creative self and my spirit. Nobody else knows how I'm really feeling, because I was taught to hide my feelings as a kid and I've done a great job, even hiding them from myself. But through the writing I'm able to start reconnecting to who I really am and it's scary and exciting at the same time. I'm discovering many selves I never knew existed before writing about them. I write to create a safety net for my dreams and hopes and desires. I put my fantasies and stories by using words and they come alive.

I write because I see possibilities and dreams that can come true. When I write, I create worlds and people and environments, where I play god and where I am Master of the Universe. I can be all the characters especially the hero and the villain, at the same time.

I write to connect to my inner world without which I'd be less than who I really am and who I want to become. I write to live."

After he finished reading he said, "I'm glad I did this exercise because it got me back in touch with what motivated me to write in the first place. Although I'd still like to sell this second novel, money and sales are not my main motivation for writing."

Paul realized his true reasons for writing: that he was motivated to write novels because he had something to share with the world and because he loved writing.

Shrink Rap

I write it my way and it's what I need to say. I'm a motivated writer who writes each and every day.

Creativity Chronicle

"The smallest action is better than the largest plan."
—JOHN GROVES

Write for twenty minutes on the subject "Why I Write."

Read over what you've written. Do your reasons for writing motivate you enough to keep on writing, even in the face of rejection, criticism, and doubt?

SHRINK WRAP-UP: UNTIL NEXT TIME

- Be certain that your reasons for writing motivate you enough to keep on writing.
- You need to find internal motivation so you can keep on writing when rejected or criticized.
- Don't rely on external motivations to write. Depend on your own reasons for being a writer.

Epilogue

"There is just one life for each of us; our own."
—EURIPIDES

Writing this book was a journey of discovery for me. It is my hope that a session, a quote, or an exercise has motivated you to continue to expand your own creative journey and achieve your artistic vision.

Remember that it's important for you to make a personal connection to what is stopping your creativity from flourishing, so you can liberate your creativity and write.

I hope by reading this book you have discovered new insights about yourself and your own creativity. Use this book to encourage, support, and nurture you. Let it inspire your creative source, which is a fountain of beauty and art flowing inside of you.

As you read this book, written from my heart, let it touch your heart. Let it motivate you to have the courage and confidence to take the risk to write what you know and to reveal to the universe who you are—a unique creative spirit.

About the Author

Referred to in the *Los Angeles Times* as "Doc Hollywood," Rachel Ballon, Ph.D., is a highly recognized creativity coach, international writing consultant, teacher, and licensed psychotherapist who specializes in writers' personal and professional issues such as overcoming fear of success, procrastination, and writers' block, while helping writers increase motivation, productivity, and creativity.

A popular workshop leader and motivational speaker, Dr. Ballon resides in Los Angeles, where she has a private practice helping writers and other creative professionals realize their artistic and creative potential. She is a screenwriter with produced television credits and a member of the Writer's Guild of America West. Dr. Ballon is the author of five widely acclaimed books: *Blueprint for Writing, The Writers' Sourcebook, Breathing Life into Your Characters, Blueprint for Screenwriting,* and *The Writer's Portable Therapist.*

Dr. Ballon is available for speaking engagements, workshops, conferences, private consultations, and counseling. She can be reached through her Web site, online at *www.rachelballon.com,* or you can e-mail her for further information regarding her services at www.*rachwrite@aol.com.*

Rachel would appreciate a review of *Unlock the Blocks* if you would like to write one. Thanking you in advance.